THE

WOO
WOO
WAY

You are a star
Right where you are
Shine Brightly!
♡ Sandy Evenson

Advance Praise

Sandy Evenson fills *The Woo Woo Way* with priceless wisdom, knowledge, heart, and understanding—a training book for overcoming obstacles that prevent us from seeing our true light. Adding to our quality of life and written for everyone, in *The Woo Woo Way,* Sandy helps you build self-trust and clearly shows you how to unlock your full potential. She guides you to find your path to the best life possible.

—**Geno Stampora,** Consultant and Coach

Our health and happiness are deeply intertwined. Unfortunately, in the United States, we have created a culture where many think health and happiness should come to them passively, with minimal self-engagement. In her book, *The Woo Woo Way,* Sandy Evenson gives the reader learnings to understand and, most importantly, tools and approaches to actively engage and create a healthier and happier life. This book will positively change lives!

—**Dr. Brian Justice,** Chiropractor, Adjunct Professor of Public Health Sciences at the Univ. of Rochester School of Medicine, Medical Director at a large insurance plan, and Chief Innovation Officer at Spine Care Partners, LLC

My hope for any woman is to connect with Sandy Evenson and allow her to guide you to a life filled with more joy and richness than you could have ever imagined. She has consistently guided me through my career and life, lovingly lifting me onto her shoulders so I could "see" the possibilities waiting for me. Sandy, with her wisdom and love, has transformed my life.

—**Wanda Stump Bupp,** Owner of The Thrill On The Hill Salon

It's not what you believe, it's how hard you believe it. Sandy believes woo to her core. Sandy walks it. And now, with *The Woo Woo Way*, she's sharing it with you. Woo is the magic of Sandy. *The Woo Woo Way* is a Manifestation Map of how to get to where you want to go. Sandy dialogues with you about where you find yourself, how you feel about being there, and how to get to where you want to be. And with the powerful stories of her journey from there to here and glimpses into her clients' struggles and breakthroughs, Sandy and woo give you the tools to uncover, honor, and transform the way of you, the way you choose to show up, and the way to step consciously into and stay true to your woo woo way.

—**Kay Walker,** Life Support Coach
Senior Coaching Skills Facilitator with Margaret Lynch Raniere

Anyone looking to unfreeze and go deep to the roots must go through this book, whether you are a coach, flooded with lots of self-development methods, or embarking on this journey to get to know yourself! I love how amazingly it depicts the "go, go, always busy" phase, rampant in daily life, of many people walking around with anxiety while having no clue about it. The stories and deepening of the teachings via tales make your book unique. This profound work and system you describe is the holy grail of finally getting out of defense and stepping into the soul mission! Want to go to the roots? This book will meet you there to blossom into your unique flower. Well done. I love how the root chakras and nervous system work together. It is a game changer, and I feel more in my body than before. I love this work. Thank you for being on my healing journey.

—**Marie Sophia Rose**

Positive thinking and positive affirmations pretty much got me nowhere. If that sounds familiar, then *The Woo Woo Way* is a must-read for any woman seeking to make life changes. With relatable stories, practical information, and an easy-to-follow playbook, Sandy Evenson guides the reader to a more empowered way of living.

—**Irene Jorgensen,** Author and Coach
A Second-Chance Friendship Cozy Mystery Series

In *The Woo Woo Way*, Sandy Evenson introduces you to the House of You and shows you how to become an exquisite "interior designer" who knows how to make the most of each "room." With plenty of stories, examples, and actionable ideas on creating a "home" that reflects who you truly are, *The Woo Woo Way* may become one of your favorite reference books for redesigning your life.
—**Penny Plautz**, author
Coming Clean: 6 Steps to Making AMENDS With Your Body
Body Confidence from the Inside Out
comingcleancoaching.com

I love, love, love *The Woo Woo Way* by Sandy Evenson. The author has created a peaceful and clear book for her reader. It is incredibly helpful how she outlines each chakra's purpose and back story, then makes it come alive with relevant and valuable stories. Her narrative is insightful and powerful. This book is a must-read for personal development beginners and experts alike. I know that these principles are pivotal. Besides, Evenson has made it so easy to access.
—**Priya Rana Kapoor,** MMFT, Coach, Speaker, and Author, Permission Media, Inc.

For anyone who's ever wondered whether they can convert nervous energy to productive thinking and action, *The Woo Woo Way* is an eye-opener. In an appealing, accessible collection of stories and theories, author Sandy Evenson shows the reader how to use EFT (Emotional Freedom Technique) to unleash stored emotional and physical pain and open the door to a more vibrant, satisfying life. Just as acupuncture and acupressure target the body's energy meridians, EFT tapping gently stimulates energy points on the body. At the same time, the subject consciously focuses on troubling or uncomfortable thoughts or emotions. In her friendly, down-to-earth manner, Evenson describes how weaving EFT tapping into her coaching work supports her clients in transforming their stored hurts and fears into a brighter, healthier, anxiety-free future.
—**Rose Benz Ericson,** Author
The Conscious Consumer: Promoting Economic Justice Through Fair Trade

You want to give this Woo Woo stuff a proper go, but after trying manifestation (whatever that means), affirmations, and so-called secret codes, you're wondering if it's all a hoax or if there's just something wrong with you. Before you give up on your big dreams or resign yourself to being stuck in a pile of suck forever, pick up *The Woo Woo Way*. Sandy Evenson takes the mystery out of our energy system by introducing us to the chakras from the perspective of how they can either help or hinder our progress. Using this combination of practical exercises and ancient wisdom, you'll finally see and release the exact patterns holding you back from experiencing the flow we all hope is waiting for us (but so rarely is) on the other side of that next yoga class or moon circle.

—**Wendy Windle,** The Love Your Bloody Self Coach

The Woo Woo Way is the perfect complement to anyone familiar with Anodea Judith and Cyndi Dale. Sandy brings a unique viewpoint of the chakras and intertwines relatable stories she and her clients experienced. I was blown away by the illustrative examples comparing the chakras to various parts of a house, such as the crown chakra as the stargazer deck—exactly as I "see" it. *The Woo Woo Way* is a wonderful book that was tough to put down!

—**Arden Reece**
Founder of ardenreececolor.com

If you are ready to heal and transform your life, it's the magic of serendipity that you've picked up this book! Sandy's relatable and actionable tools and processes will help you release the blocks that keep you stuck and unleash your inner power to live your life with unshakable confidence and joyful exuberance. The time is now, and this book is the answer. I LOVE *The Woo Woo Way*. It will change your life.

—**Fiona Orr**, EPIC Life Coach
Creator of *The Magical Manifestation Formula* and *The Epic Stance*

Coach Sandy Evenson shares her heart and wisdom with us in *The Woo Woo Way*. Her honesty is touching as she describes the real struggles of her own and others on a transformational journey. This profound insight allows her to guide her clients and the reader through a liberating process. I have found her method to have a positive and therapeutic impact on my life, releasing me from the past and helping me discover my true self.
—**Coach Rosa Smith-Montanaro**
Best-Selling Author, *Mind Over Platter*

The Woo Woo Way is a must-read for women seeking transformational change. Sandy Evenson provides guidance to help them transform their lives and become the best version of themselves. When you open up the chakras, miracles can emerge that one never thought could occur. Sandy's guidance is life-changing and will help improve lives.
—**Kandiee Campbell**, MA, LMHC, CEO
of Awaken Tranquility, LLC

The Woo Woo Way is more than a book! It's an experience! The stories at the beginning of each chapter make Sandy's wisdom come alive. All you need to do is open a chapter, read the first five words, let them hook you, and dive into the rest of the chapter for an inner journey. You will come out of it refreshed and wiser. What an experience!
—**Nathalie ten Have-Fradin,** Mindvalley Holobody
and 10X Fitness Coach at nathalieu.com

When you've done everything for everyone else and still feel unfulfilled, find your path to self-discovery with *The Woo Woo Way*. Tangible explanations of the body's energy systems artfully pair with evidence-based techniques to unblock emotional baggage from the body. Read this book to let go of what's holding you back and transform your life.
—**Patricia C. Rogers,** CST-D
Advanced CranioSacral Therapist and Owner of Body Smarts™

The Woo Woo Way is a must-read for women waking up to their lives and thinking, "there must be more for me." There is. Sandy Evenson gives you a map to find your missing pieces in The House of You. With relatable stories, practical information, and easy-to-follow meditations, this book distills centuries of wisdom and ushers in a new generation of women's empowerment and manifestation.
—**Julie Colvin,** Director of Wellness Writers Press

THE WOO WOO WAY

Unblock Your Chakras and Transform Your Life

SANDY EVENSON

Goodyear, Arizona

First published in the USA in 2023 by Sandy Evenson

Paperback ISBN: 978-1-958405-62-8
Hardcover ISBN: 978-1-958405-63-5
eBook ISBN: 978-1-958405-61-1
Library of Congress Control Number: Number: 2023902040

Publishing House: Spotlight Publishing House™ in Goodyear, AZ
https://spotlightpublishinghouse.com
Marketing Visibility: Maggie Mongan, Brilliant Breakthroughs, Inc.
Developmental Editor: Cindy Childress, Founder and Owner of Childress Business Communications
Editor: Lynn Thompson, Living on Purpose Communications
Portraits: Blair Hornbuckle, BlairHornbuckle.com
Book Cover: Patsy Balacchi of Zenotica.com, and Angie Ayala
Interior Design: Marigold2k

For information, contact: sandy@sandyevenson.com
Instagram: @coachsandyevenson
Facebook: Coach Sandy Evenson
LinkedIn: Coach Sandy Evenson
YouTube: Sandy Evenson Coaching

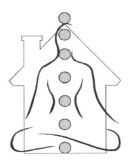

Dedication

Dear wise, ageless woman. I wrote this book for you.
Let the stories, lessons, and exercises I share bring you
the peace, joy, and clarity you seek.
This is your time. Reclaim your authentic inner power.
Unblock your chakras and transform your life.

Welcome to The Woo Woo Way
https://youtu.be/xfu8dDI179k

SCAN ME

Contents

Foreword

"I want to write a book," Sandy Evenson told me. We met in Helena Bowen's TEDx speaker course and connected on many levels. The following year, she signed up for my Success Story class, where she first wrote many of the stories in *The Woo Woo Way*. Every week she submitted another story that made me laugh or cry—sometimes both. There was no doubt in my mind that she had an important book to write.

Later on, we worked together closely through my book writing course. While many students struggled with inner critics, imposter syndrome, or old-fashioned "writer's block," Sandy rarely did. That's because she had access to many of the tools in this book, so when she hit roadblocks, she knew exactly how to get past them. Instead, her dilemma was often, "What goes in this book, and what goes in other, future books?" Finally, she crafted your reading experience in this book focused on tapping, chakras, and shadows. And I couldn't be more impressed by the work she has done.

Sandy has written a groundbreaking, life-changing book for anyone ready to take a walk on the "woo woo" side. With the art of a poet, she presents the metaphor of a house for the chakras, which helped me understand the relationships between the chakras in a fresh way. And Sandy doesn't shy away from the challenges we face in life, especially as women—finding our voice, being a caretaker, carrying grief, shame, anxiety, and anger—which we can barely admit even to ourselves.

Shortly after editing the Heart Chakra chapter, I applied Sandy's teaching. I was in line at a Starbucks, and the woman in front of me was taking *forever*. She marveled at the number of food choices and asked in detail about the difference between a decaf Americano and decaf drip coffee. "It's all decaf," I wanted to say. Instead, my chest tightened, and I felt my throat close. That's when I realized I was getting mad. *I refuse to waste my energy on her,* I thought. I pulled out my phone to distract myself and had a revelation. This situation was just what Sandy wrote about—when people get under our skin, they often remind us of something in ourselves.

So, I started tapping my fingers on my thigh (another tidbit from Sandy for when you need to tap in public) and let my inner critic run its course. *She's taking up too much time. How does she not know how to act in a Starbucks line? It seems like she hasn't ordered coffee in 20 years. There are people behind me. She's so selfish.* With all that judgment released, I noticed that she acted like her inner child was in charge—demanding attention and needing help. Here's the jaw-dropper: *Wasn't it true,* I thought, *that when I'm in an unfamiliar setting doing something new, sometimes I need more time, more help? And in those times, isn't it amazing to get what I need?* I felt my anger dissolving. The barista was laughing with the woman and didn't seem irritated. *Maybe it was just me.*

Then, she pulled out her phone to pay from the Starbucks app. At first, she couldn't find the app, and the barista offered to help. Oh, then she couldn't log in.

"Let me get this for you," I said. "Pay it forward."

She turned around and flashed me an enormous smile. "Thank you! That's amazing," she said. Then, she thanked me again twice while we were in line for our orders. The last time, I replied, "You just never know when something really good is about to happen."

With Sandy's tools, you really don't have to sweat the small things. And even with the big things life throws at you, something good is right around the corner when you follow *The Woo Woo Way*. Each story in this book shows you how others have done it, and you can, too. Keep reading. You're in good hands with Sandy.

—Cindy Childress, PhD

Preface

Welcome, Seeker

You're entering the world of woo. You may be a curious newcomer, wondering, *What the heck are chakras anyway?* Perhaps you have passed this way before. Or maybe you have a lifetime pass to woo, and your knowledge of chakras is broad.

Whatever your path has been up to this point, one thing is clear: *Now is your time.* You've spent your whole life making sure everyone else is happy and supporting them. Trying not to take up too much space, not to be too loud, and bending over backward to get along while dealing with aches, pains, and medical mysteries, you feel like things should be better by now.

Then, you woke up to a new idea. Instead of waiting for your life to change or resigning yourself to your lot, you transform. Being your authentic self is your birthright, and you claim it.

Regardless of your reasons for being here, enter with a beginner's mind. And be open to a new way of seeing and being: *The Woo Woo Way.*

Why Woo Woo?

As the saying goes, *when the student is ready, the teacher appears.*

Some might call it chance, luck, or coincidence that right when you're ready to learn something, the path forward falls into your lap.

I call it "serendipity." The hidden world of woo dropped into my life when I needed it most.

At first, a part of me felt apprehensive. An image of the Ouija board popped into my head. And Sister Mary Somebody's warnings echoed in my ear. "Stay away from that. It's the devil's doorway." However, she only made me smile. My inner science geek prevailed. I didn't mind the skeptics who said EFT (Emotional Freedom Technique) was too far "out there." Without knowing much about the field of energy medicine, they thought it wasn't plausible. And they called it "woo woo." Nevertheless, I embraced it.

A new adventure unfolded as I uncovered long-repressed or never recognized parts of me. These elements blocked my powerful chakra energy and kept me stuck. Yet, these unconscious blocks held precious gifts. They were hiding in the shadows behind the wounds of my past. Unblocking my chakras cleared the way for strengths beyond belief to surface.

This inner journey ignited a passion in me to help other women empower themselves. My heart was bursting to share empowerment and manifestation processes. I deeply believed others, too, could heal and transform their lives.

In popular psychology, "manifestation" refers to self-help strategies to help us achieve our goals. Most techniques tell us to center our thoughts primarily on our desired outcomes. And affirmations are used to help us keep our focus on the goal. Our thoughts and affirmations are an integral part of what's known as The Law of Attraction. In essence, our thoughts, good or bad, become reality. However, there's often something hindering the manifestation process. In Chapter Three, I explain why our affirmations seem to fall flat. And we are left still yearning for the manifestation of our goals and dreams.

How does that land for you? If you're like many of my early contacts, when I would say, "transformation," they'd barely resist the urge to roll their eyes. I felt certain they were thinking, "Oh, Lord, there she goes again."

Then, over time, as they watched me change and grow, woo seemed like possibly the one thing they hadn't tried that might work to enhance their life experience. As a result, interest in my coaching work grew one by one as people considered what could improve in their lives with my seemingly strange approach. In this book, I share the foundational knowledge that underlies my coaching and helps you shine your best life.

Sandy Evenson
Rochester, New York

We are integrated multi-dimensional beings
made of pure energy. And the degree to which we know
this truth about ourselves is the degree to which
we live either in pain or in bliss.
—Dr. Sue Mortar, *The Energy Codes*

Introduction

More than a typical self-help book, *The Woo Woo Way* is a guide to unleashing your inner power. It's a path of self-discovery and empowerment where manifesting your dreams is possible. In this book, I share stories, lessons, and bits of wisdom from my travels along the woo woo path. While reading, you may experience an epiphany or two, which is what I call a divine aha moment. And with each one, shifts you thought impossible occur.

This book is about your mind and body—and also your spirit. Transforming your life and living to your highest potential requires embracing a higher power. Your choice may be nature, science, mathematics, Buddha, Allah, Jesus, Mohamed, or the Force. I refer to Spirit, Source, The Universe, God, The Conscious Universe, and The Divine. Likewise, I also address your inner being, comprised of the Self, the Shadow Self, aka, the Ego, and the Higher Self—your Soul. When you clear your chakras, you gain a new perspective on life. You see the world through the eyes of the neutral observer, your Higher Self. And you feel closer to Divine presence.

Read *The Woo Woo Way* from front to back as a progressive journey through the chakras. If you're more advanced, you may choose to do intensive work on a particular chakra. You can always return to the chakras for specific issues and concerns with this book as your reference guide.

The first three chapters lay the foundation of my teachings: tapping, chakras, and shadows. Then we put it all together and apply these tools to each chakra from 1st to 7th or Root to Crown. You learn what to look for if a certain chakra is blocked and how to unblock it.

I find it helpful to take this journey with a metaphor of renovating a house. I call it The House of You. The end of each chakra chapter includes an Architect's Note from that part of the house. These quick references remind you of the purpose and function of each chakra so you can keep them flowing smoothly.

The Woo Woo Way also contains my personal and client stories. Within them are examples of profound epiphanies and transformation. For my clients' safety, I put all except one in *witness protection* for their privacy. Their names, locations, occupations, and other identifiable traits are changed. While I've altered the other people and circumstances in their stories, the overall lessons are intact. As you read these stories, think of times when you've had similar challenges or how your experiences are different.

Watch for the URL links and QR codes in the book. I invite you to read along with me or close your eyes and listen to the messages from The House of You. In addition, I recorded all of *Your Woo Woo Way Playbook* in audio-video segments as my gift to you. Tap along with me. Close your eyes and I'll guide you through the visualizations and tapping.

Your Woo Woo Way Playbook – Homeplay

I'm not a fan of the term, "homework." The word itself emotes drudgery. It's work, pronounced, *were-errk*. We often say we *have to* work, and we *get to* play. I merged these two ideas to create *Your Woo Woo Way Playbook*, which is chock-full of homeplay—rather than homework. *Your Playbook* with self-guided activities is in the back of this book.

You get to choose the pace of your inner work to clear emotional blocks in a way that feels safe. *Your Playbook* includes tapping, visualization, meditation, and other chakra-balancing exercises. Do customize the activities to your needs. After your first read-through, revisit the exercises often as you unblock your chakras layer by layer.

If there's something I suggest that sounds too "out there," it's okay. I felt the same when I first tried tapping, as I share in Chapter One. And that's the beauty of it. You can still feel an impact, even if you don't fully believe. So, be open to doing things that might feel silly and see what shifts for you.

Sometimes a sensitive topic might trigger you or remind you of something in your past. This memory can activate old emotions and touch a sore spot. When this happens, pause, take a breath, and use the tools in *Your Playbook* until you feel a shift. The more you practice the homeplays, the safer you feel when rough memories arise.

Almost every book I own contains my underlines, circles, and highlights. You might do that too. Bringing your own stories to the surface is helpful as you do your homeplay and journaling.

Writing is one of the best ways to connect with your inner being. Along the way, different aspects of yourself come forward. What these internal parts of you teach is gold. Capture divine aha moments, thoughts, and emotions in your journal. You may even create affirmations and tapping scripts based on your writing.

Use this Book as an Oracle

Anything can be an oracle. Bibliomancy, receiving messages from books, is practiced around the world. The most common books people use are sacred, such as the Bible, Torah, and I Ching.

Begin with an open-ended question, for example, "What do I need to know about this situation?" Then, open this book and flip to a random page. Make a note of the chakra or topic, and choose what resonates with you. It can be one word, phrase, or paragraph. This message from Spirit is for you, a hug from the Universe.

May the lessons I share inspire you to trust in the process of unblocking your chakras. Come along with me on The Woo Woo Way. Transform your life and manifest your dreams.

Let's Do It

Let's write
a story.

Who shall we be?
Where shall we go?

Let's do it

Together.

—Ray Justice, *Spiritual Arousal*

Chapter One

Tapping into Healing Begins

The Whispered Cry

March 12, 2013, pre-dawn, Rincon, Georgia, Lost Plantation Golf Course 20 miles outside of Savannah

"Come on, Josie. Let's go," I called. My cocker spaniel came running, and we went out the door into the early morning chill. She sprinted ahead of me, raring to go. I didn't mind walking her. It was my time to be alone, engrossed in nature and my thoughts. The two of us moved along the edge of the golf course in that still, quiet, magical hour just before first light. Josie stopped to sniff and squatted to leave the first of many pee-mails for other dogs and critters to find. Her thick, curly fur shone under the streetlight. My own curls blew into my face. I laughed and said, "Geez, Josie, I've become one of those dog-look-alike women."

Worrisome thoughts drifted into my headspace, and I lost my smile. I stopped, looked up at the bright stars piercing the black velvet sky and let out a whispered cry. I gasped and sobbed, "Dear God and Holy Universe, please help me. I can't do this anymore. It's too hard. I don't know what to do. I'm ready for this to be over."

Josie sensed the shift in my energy and grew impatient, jerking me out of my lament on my end of the leash and lunged ahead, nose to the ground. I wiped the salty tears from my face and trudged along behind her.

Just keep walking, keep breathing. Shake it off. Get it together.

To the outside world, I appeared happy. I was a successful hairstylist in love with what I did, who I did it for, and whom I did it with—my salon professional colleagues.

On the inside, it was a different story. In truth, I was in turmoil about my husband, Dennis. His mental and physical health worried me every day because I never knew what state he'd be in when I returned home from work.

I was a total wreck—hanging out with my perpetual companions, fear and anxiety. The constant voice in my mind that I now recognize as my inner critic badgered me. I beat myself up over the mess I'd made of my life. Witnessing my husband's descent into the dark night of his weary soul seared my heart. To numb the pain of PTSD (post-traumatic stress disorder), Dennis self-medicated with drugs and alcohol, which only served to exacerbate his anxiety and depression. Then, I became the target of his pent-up frustration and anger at the world. His rage-filled rants were loud, his shouts deafening. And still, I told no one. I felt alone and scared.

Be Careful What You Pray For

Two days after begging God and the Holy Universe for help during that tearful dog walk, I came home from work to find Dennis sitting in his favorite spot on the couch with his head bowed. The cushion beneath him sagged three inches below the others. Dennis raised his head and looked at me. He balanced a large plastic bowl between his legs with what appeared to be dark specks of red wine floating in clear, water-like fluid.

"I'm sick," he said. Dennis was weak. Yet it was impossible to get him to settle down. His recent diagnosis of episodic dementia kicked into overdrive. The night dragged on into one long, hellish nightmare.

Dennis couldn't stay in bed for more than a few minutes. Neither of us slept. As the night wore on, he grew weaker and collapsed on the floor. I dialed 911, and the ambulance whisked him away.

The ambulance attendants took Dennis to Emergency, ending up in the intensive care unit (ICU). And those red specks in the bowl? Blood. His excessive alcohol use caused an internal bleed, worsened by the blood thinner for his heart condition. At first, there were life-threatening critical events almost every hour. I'm sparing you the gory details. However, the medical insanity continued over several weeks and months.

One day, amid this chaos, I received an email newsletter from Hay House recommending a new book, *The Tapping Solution,* by Nick Ortner. Nick espoused science-based evidence on the effectiveness of the Emotional Freedom Technique (EFT), or "tapping." The flyer boasted that over a hundred clinical peer reviewed studies demonstrate how EFT turns off our fight or flight stress response. Additionally, Nick described the positive impact that tapping has on emotional and physical stress, anxiety, pain, illness, and PTSD.

My stress level is beyond measure. Maybe this can help me.

I ordered the book and immediately received two free downloadable tapping audios. Meanwhile, the voice of Dennis was echoing in my head.

Really, Sandy? You're gonna do this? You know it's crazy, right? Poking yourself in the face is nuts. You just fell for another piece of woo woo crap.

I tried it anyway.

Too anxious to sit down, I stood beside the dining room table near my laptop. The recording was called *Evening Clearing.* The soft voice of Jessica Ortner, Nick's sister, narrated the tapping exercise. Tapping my fingertips on my face and body felt weird at first.

How odd. If anybody saw me doing this, they'd think I'd gone off the deep end.

At that point, I'd try anything, though. Relief and much-needed sleep were in order, and I counted on Jessica to get me there. Ignoring negative thoughts, I tapped and repeated Jessica's words. It was uncanny how the phrases were the exact thoughts I had spinning in my head.

"This is so stressful." "I'm not doing enough." "What if I'm not doing enough?" "I'm so scared, and I don't know what to do."

Another emotion popped up as I tapped. It was guilt. A river of tears gushed from my eyes and flowed down my cheeks and onto my neck. I didn't stop. I just stayed with Jessica and expressed my emotions. Then, my body shifted into a state of calm. With a long, slow sigh, I let go of the heavy guilt. The recording ended and led right into the next one, *Evening Affirmation.* Completing both tapping sessions took only thirteen minutes.

After sleeping through the night for the first time in many years, I woke up feeling refreshed and ready to face another day.

This is incredible. I think there's something to this tapping thing.

The next day, Jessica Ortner led me through the *Morning Clearing* and *Morning Affirmation* audios. Even though I still felt tremendous stress, I functioned with more clarity and purpose.

Just put one foot in front of the other, one step at a time.

Soon after that first tapping experience, Nick announced an upcoming event, an evening interactive webinar. The topic was tapping for financial stability.

Again, my inner worrier chimed in, *well, I know I need that.*

I thought about money all the time. How would I handle everything? How do I juggle the mortgage, utilities, two car payments, and huge hospital bills? I had no clue how much our health insurance would cover. Could I afford long-term, expensive care for Dennis? Each day the list of questions grew.

Signing on to Nick's presentation that night, I joined other attendees from all over the world. We each had varying degrees of stress around money. And we were eager to hear what Nick might share.

I'm curious. Could one evening call with a bunch of strangers do anything for me and my situation?

Tapping is For Real

The next day a $1,500 check arrived in the mail.

Wait. What on Earth? This is so bizarre. I don't get how such a small amount of tapping could work. Damn, it sure seems like it did. Nah, it's got to be a coincidence. It can't be that easy. It's too out there, too woo woo, even for me.

The unexpected money came from an escrow account. It reminded me again how much I didn't know about our mortgage and all the other bills. Surprised, I thought about my tapping experience.

I've touched into something greater than me. I can do this.

I haven't even told you about the best part. The check I received was for the exact amount I needed to pay the last part of the bill from a lawyer. It didn't end there, though. The following morning, my husband's old friend and former coworker called.

"Hey, Sandy, I wanted to give you a quick heads up," she said. "You're going to get a check in the mail."

"What?" I asked in amazement. "Are you kidding me? What do you mean, a check?"

I felt her compassion as she described how a group of people who worked with Dennis wanted to do something to help. They had opened an account for donations, and they all contributed.

"You should get it in tomorrow's mail. And just so you know, it's for a thousand dollars."

I caught my breath and said, "Oh my God, really?" Emotion overtook me. "I'm speechless. My heart is full. Dennis would be thrilled to know that his coworker friends cared this much." Months passed before I could tell anyone about this kind gesture without blubbering. However, this type of thing kept happening. Money and acts of kindness continued to come to me in unforeseen ways.

Tapping is for real.

This initial tapping experience sparked my desire to learn more. My inner geeky science nerd devoured information on EFT, or tapping. Then, my self-improvement seeker side wanted to go further and deeper. I wondered what else this technique could conquer. Little did I know how valuable tapping would be for me. I never fathomed what was ahead. Tumultuous times, medical emergencies, and emotional overload continued for more than four years.

Nonetheless, tapping equipped me with a powerful mind-body tool, and I stepped onto a more solid foundation of safety and security. Impressed and touched by the power of this technique, I dove into advanced trainings and transformational life coach certification.

The Magic of Working With Energy

Before the ambulance siren blared Dennis to the hospital that night, when I felt the world crashing down around me, standing strong wasn't in my wheelhouse. Frozen in place with my head down, I felt too afraid to make a change. For many years, I explored self-improvement. Finally, however, that traumatic answer to my fretful, whispered cry for help forced me to choose. I knew I had to show up, put one foot in front of the other, hour by hour, day by day. Ultimately, something deep within me was shifting, exposing a tiny bit of inner strength, self-courage, and the taste of freedom to be me.

I felt touched by magic after listening to Nick Ortner and Jessica Ortner. The EFT tapping they taught me combines ancient acupuncture principles with modern psychology. All you need to perform this self-administered technique is your fingertips. You tap acupressure points on your face and body while expressing any negative thoughts and feelings. Tapping sends a signal to your brain, turning off the stress response known as fight, flight, or freeze. It's used worldwide for many issues, such as fear, anxiety, pain, trauma, and performance. Safe and effective, tapping can be performed by anyone, anywhere, and at any time.

Tapping helped me break the constant cycle of over-giving and self-neglect. Like me, many women often do everything and anything for everyone else. Yet we fail to do the same for ourselves. Then, our thoughts spin and overload our emotions. We deplete our energy worrying about our health, weight issues, or foggy brains. We feel like we're falling apart in body, mind, and spirit. We say to ourselves, *I thought things would be different. When is it my turn?*

Tapping is like flipping a switch, a nervous system electrical disconnect. In an instant, it turns off the fight or flight stress response and lowers anxiety. The frenetic thoughts in our minds immediately calm down, giving us more clarity and focus. It's important to allow ourselves to feel all our emotions. Participating in private or group coaching sessions for EFT work allows us to discover just where we hold the wounds of our past. We move stuck energy by uncovering the hidden blocks in our chakras. And that's when the magic of dramatic transformational healing begins.

Your turn is now. I can verify that it's never too late to change. We have the power to thrive as the loving, joy-filled women we were born to be. Even if you think it's too woo woo, hear me out. I promise to teach you how to clear your innermost blocks safely.

Within the pages of this book, I demonstrate how tapping reduces stress and revitalizes our energy. Along with learning more about tapping, I invite you to join me on a transformational journey. I'm your guide on exploring the seven major energy centers in our bodies, known as chakras. As you uncover hidden secrets, you gain deeper understanding of your most challenging issues. You *can* heal the wounds of your past and move forward toward your goals and dreams. Each of us is born with a natural flow of empowerment and manifestation energy managed by our chakras.

"Chakras," a Sanskrit word that means "wheel" or "cycle," are positioned along the spine, from the base (root) to the crown of your head. They support energy channels called meridians that nourish your body and affect every bodily function, including your organs, nervous system, and brain. And the tapping points used in EFT are located on meridian endpoints.

In Chapter Two, I describe each of the seven chakras, their specific purposes, and how each works independently of the others. Together, they regulate the flow of your *inner energy*. The state of your chakras (and whether the energy channels are open or blocked) impacts your entire energy system. Regardless of your endeavors, you can uncover the hidden blocks to your success. Learning the core concepts of each chakra helps you unleash this energetic power within. By unblocking your chakras, you can reclaim your birthright of living in authenticity and joy.

In her book, *Unblocked,* Margaret Lynch Raniere states that every outer problem, struggle, or complaint has an inner root cause. Therefore, learning about your internal energy system and the seven major chakras is crucial. Through my stories and teachings, I show you how and why this energy flow gets clogged and shut down, blocking the chakras. Instead of continuing to be full of self-doubt and destined to repeat the same mistakes, join me in tapping to move through the chakras and release trapped energy. I share a taste of the woo woo experience to help keep your chakra energy flowing.

Using the tapping homeplay exercises in *Your Playbook*, you can tap any time you feel triggered by something. Voice the nasty negative stuff that's swirling in your head. It could be the first time you express these thoughts and feelings aloud. Perhaps they are words you'd never say out loud or in public. Maybe they were taboo in your home environment or culture. That's why I recommend finding a quiet space to tap where you won't be disturbed or interrupted.

As I said, you can tap anywhere. You can walk and tap while saying the words to yourself or out loud. Escaping to the bathroom for a few minutes to tap and defuse stress works wonders. And your car is a perfect place to tap, rant, and scream. First, tap the side of your hand on the steering wheel while driving. Then, tap on your face and body at red lights and stop signs. Smile and control your temper with tapping. Instead of giving somebody the finger for cutting you off, point your fingers at yourself and tap.

We discover and pinpoint our obstacles by using visualization and tapping. Then the power within us is released as we clear the blockages in our chakras. As you've probably guessed, there's a distinct link between our emotions and the chakras. In the next chapter, you discover how to unblock your chakras and release the energies of empowerment and manifestation. The architect's blueprint reveals your powerful energy system and the chakras in detail so you can finally be at home in your empowered brilliance—shining in The House of You. *Your wildest dreams are waiting.*

You can't hate yourself happy,
You can't criticize yourself thin,
You can't shame yourself wealthy.
Real change begins with self-love and self-care.
—Jessica Ortner
The Tapping Solution for Weight-Loss and Body Confidence

Check out the Tapping tutorials and graphic:

What is EFT Tapping?
https://youtu.be/E_3npLJiUjg

How to Tap
https://youtu.be/YbwIRdcJOv8

SCAN ME

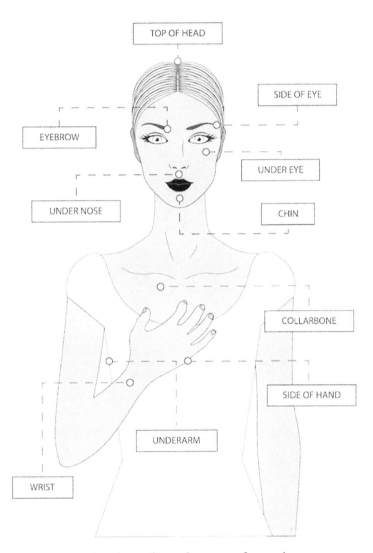

Customized graphic design by Arden Reece for sandyevenson.com

Chapter Two

On Shaky Ground

The Starter Home

Easter Sunday, 1977, Alexandria, Virginia

"Oh my God, Dennis, come here. You've got to see this," I shouted to my husband.

"What's going on?" Dennis yelled back as he walked up the hall from the bedroom.

"Look," I said, half-crying. "We need paint now."

"Holy crap. What the hell?" Dennis said as he raised his hand to form a visor over his eyes.

We stood there in shock. Early morning sunbeams bounced off the walls as they streamed through the curtain-less large picture window. Feeling sick to my stomach, I sighed and said, "I never imagined it could look like this."

We made a mistake. It was our first home purchase. And the only time we could view the house was after work at night when the walls appeared as soft, golden yellow, and the carpet, a burnt orange. Even though it wasn't my choice, I could work with it. However, in that moment, all my interior decorating ideas melted away. Everywhere we looked in the open floor plan space was painted a bright, electric, day-glow yellow. The carpet turned out to be bright orange. The '70s color scheme continued in the kitchen with yellow countertops and flooring. And wait for it, the appliances were olive green, and the pantry, chartreuse. People told us to be sure to look at houses when it's been raining. Who knew we had to worry about sunshine?

A couple of gallons of white paint and various other changes rectified the glare. Then, I found our second first-time buyers' mistake in the tiny bathroom. Never mind the mass of little pink roses surrounding the pink tub, sink, and toilet. It was the only bathroom in the house, which was no big deal; we'd both grown up in homes with just one bathroom. However, we had to string an extension cord down the hall in this house. There wasn't an electrical outlet.

How did I not see that?

Then, another surprise awaited us. We removed the tub to replace it with an enclosed shower. The only thing beneath it was dirt. The foundation was missing.

Are you kidding me?

And to top it off, several old whiskey jugs poked out of the ground where cement should've been.

Well, that explains a lot.

Looking back at that house, I see tangible signs of instability in our lives. Dennis and I each had internal weaknesses under our deep love for each other. The two of us stood on shaky ground. I spent years trying to plaster over the cracks in our foundation. Yet, I didn't know what to do about it, and I was too afraid to try. Treading water, I relied on self-improvement books, recordings, and seminars to keep me afloat.

I survived chaos with tapping, as I describe in Chapter One. Convinced by the amazing results, it hooked me as soon as I tried it. Are you intrigued by this weird-looking emotional healing method?

Perhaps discovering the invisible energy system in your body gives you hope. It's never too late to live the life you desire. I was over sixty when I discovered tapping and how it works to unblock energy through the chakras. To launch that journey for you, please meet the architect of The House of You.

The Architect's Blueprint

The Architect has many names, including, though not limited to, God, Spirit, The Conscious Universe, Source, or our Higher Power. Whichever name suits you best, think of that Creator as your Architect designing your House of You blueprint. As you understand your original design, you discover opportunities for inner self-renovations. Unearthing the gifts buried under the crumbling structure can help us regain control of our lives—like finding hardwood floors under the carpet—beauty that's been there all along and revealed during renovation.

With me as your professional home inspector, we take a step-by-step walkthrough of our inner selves. As we uncover blocks in your energetic flow, I show you how to break through the old built-up gunk. Then, you emerge less stressed, more energized, and empowered to shine your best self.

We move through The House of You on a tour of the seven major energy centers, the chakras. While they are invisible to us, we sense their energy. For example, when we fall in love, we feel our Heart Chakra radiate positive vibrations. And if we lose that love, we feel a broken heart's lower vibrational, searing pain.

Inner energy runs through our bodies like the electrical system in a house. We tend to take it for granted when it runs in the background with efficiency. However, if a circuit breaker gets blown, we lose power to several outlets within the home, causing an entire room or whole house to go dark. All supporting functions stop—for heat, air, and water. In a similar way, our inner house of power can get shut down.

The House of You Inner Renovation Project

Let's take a virtual tour of a home renovation project through my innovative approach to teaching chakras. Our bottom-to-top inspection of the house areas reveals the seven major chakras. (Chapters Four through Ten explore each chakra in detail.) To illustrate the seven levels of chakras in the body, I picture a metaphorical home renovation. The house you envision is unique to you. For example, substitute a garage or shed if you have never had a basement.

As you read each chapter of this book, imagine a house suitable for you. Let the house metaphor help locate specific chakras in your body. Then, using your inner vision, remove blockages and reclaim potent gifts while renovating The House of You. Allow your subconscious mind to show you what you need to see. Reclaiming our inner power to manifest our best lives is comparable to renovating an old house. How much refurbishing do you think your internal house needs?

When we examine a house, it might seem to have what realtors call "good bones." However, what damaging mishaps might we find long hidden and neglected? What's under the floorboards, behind the walls, under the sink, in the basement or attic? Is it safe to explore the structure? If we don't like some of its interior design, how can we improve it?

Clogs in the plumbing can cause real problems in a home. Likewise, chakras act as pipe valves in our energy system. And the inner power we were born with is suppressed when our energy centers, the chakras, are blocked.

We must shine a light in the dark places, rewire the electrical system, and get the pipes cleared, so fuel, air, water, and power can flow freely. Consider me your guide as we inspect the structure and strength of our inner energy centers, the chakras.

Empowerment and Manifestation Channels

Our energy centers, the chakras, regulate our inner energy system. For example, our lower four chakras control the upward flow of empowerment energy from the Root to the Heart Chakra. And our upper chakras manage the manifestation energy flowing down from the Crown to the Heart Chakra.

As each chakra comes online throughout the phases of our childhood development, our innate inner power grows and strengthens. However, our chakras can become blocked during the growth stages. It happens most often when parental or caretaking support is lacking, which impedes each successive chakra. In that case, the flow of energy can't move through our system, hinders our emotional growth, and affects our bodies, minds, and spirits.

Want to see how all your chakras work together? The Architect's Blueprint outlines each chakra from the Root (bottom) to the Crown (top) of The House of You: its affirmation, main themes, primary issue, the location where you feel it in your body, where it corresponds in the virtual home, the color resonance, wisdom crystal, and the developmental stage when the chakra comes online.

The chakras' colors and crystals help you harness energy to reinforce meditation and strengthen chakra balance. Since the wisdom crystals are my recommendations, go with your intuition to choose any crystal in that chakra color to aid in clearing the chakra's blocked energy. Enhance vitality by including those colors in your clothing and home décor. The crystals can be worn, held in your hand, carried in a pocket, or placed near you.

The blueprint for each chakra is available in the aligned chapters of *Your Woo Woo Way Playbook* for easy reference. Meanwhile, notice how the functions shift from one chakra to the next and which colors or parts draw you the most.

The Seven Primary Chakras

1st Chakra

Name: Root

Affirmation: I Am

My Right: To Be Here

Themes: Empowered Stability, Energy, Comfort, Safety, Security

Primary Issues: Safety, Security, and Survival

Location in the Body: Base of the Spine

In The House of You: The Foundation

Color Resonance: Red

Chakra Wisdom Crystal: Ruby

Developmental Stage: Womb to 18 Months

2nd Chakra

Name: Sacral

Affirmation: I Feel

My Right: To Feel and To Have

Themes: Empowered Creativity, Passion, Desires, Needs, Sensuality, Sexuality, and Sociability

Primary Issues: Sensuality, Sexuality, Emotions, and Creativity

Location in the Body: Abdomen, Just Below the Navel

In The House of You: The Basement

Color Resonance: Orange

Chakra Wisdom Crystal: Orange Carnelian

Developmental Stage: Six Months to Two Years

3rd Chakra

Name: Solar Plexus

Affirmation: I Do

My Right: To Act

Themes: Empowered Strength, Personality, Power, and Determination

Primary Issues: Power, Strength of Will, and Purpose

Location in the Body: Upper Abdomen, Just Below Ribcage

In The House of You: The Great Room

Color Resonance: Yellow

Chakra Wisdom Crystal: Citrine

Developmental Stage: Eighteen Months to Four Years

4th Chakra

Name: Heart

Affirmation: I Love

My Right: To Love

Themes: Empowered Acceptance, Love, Compassion, and Sincerity

Primary Issues: Love and Relationships

Location in the Body: Chest Area

In The House of You: The Kitchen

Color Resonance: Green

Chakra Wisdom Crystal: Emerald

Developmental Stage: Four to Seven Years

5th Chakra

Name: Throat

Affirmation: I Speak

My Right: To Speak

Themes: Empowered Communication, Expression, Inspiration, Resonance, and Voice

Primary Issues: Communication and Engagement

Location in the Body: Neck Area

In The House of You: The Mezzanine

Color Resonance: Blue

Chakra Wisdom Crystal: Sapphire

Developmental Stage: Seven to Twelve Years

6th Chakra

Name: Third Eye

Affirmation: I See

My Right: To See

Themes: Empowered Intuition, Vision, Imagination, Lucidity, Meditation, Trust, and Psychic Abilities

Primary Issues: Intuition and Imagination

Location in the Body: Brow

In The House of You: The Attic

Color Resonance: Indigo

Chakra Wisdom Crystal: Sodalite

Developmental Stage: Adolescence

7ᵗʰ Chakra

Name: Crown

Affirmation: I Understand

My Right: To Know

Themes: Empowered Wisdom, Fulfillment, Spiritual Connection, and Enlightenment

Primary Issues: Enlightenment, Spiritual Connection, and Wisdom

Location in the Body: Top of the Head

In The House of You: The Stargazer Deck

Color Resonance: Violet

Chakra Wisdom Crystal: Amethyst

Developmental Stage: Throughout Life

Seven Chakras Aligned in The House of You

Empowered alignment of all chakras, body, mind, emotions, and spirit.

Chakra Wisdom Crystal: Clear Quartz, Master Healer

Come back to this house blueprint as a reference any time you're uncertain about which chakra means what or how they connect, just like systems in a house. In time, this information becomes second nature to you. Physical sensations and feelings help you recognize stuck energy anywhere within yourself. And you know just how to clear it.

Chakra Transformational Journey

The cyclical pattern of *striving and not arriving* ended in my self-discovery that my inner house was in shambles. A personal chakra journey during coach training uncovered blocks throughout my energy system, and I saw how my beaten-down psyche affected my physical body. Meanwhile, tapping kept me grounded as I continued with self-empowerment work. Finally, going deep within, I found the girl I'd put aside so long ago. This process awakened a part of me that I had forgotten, fueling a renewed vibrancy within me. I saw visible changes in my body. And as my mind cleared, a more passionate spirit emerged.

And people noticed. "You're glowing," they'd say. "Tell me your secret. What are you doing?"

I would smile and answer, "It's not a magic pill. However, the results are magical."

Unblocking your chakras unlocks your untapped potential and much-needed self-compassion. You harness stuck energy and use it to become who you were meant to be in your original architect's blueprint. Women like us yearn to regain control of our lives. We long for optimum health, prosperity, loving relationships, and joy. You can have all those things by harvesting the power and possibility of each open chakra's free-flowing energy. Embrace this renovation journey by perceiving the chakras as integral parts of a house.

Move through the chakras from first to seventh because each builds on the strength or weaknesses of the one before. Then, similar to a home renovation, you excavate, inspect, and refurbish, room by room, chakra by chakra, to uncover and remove hidden blocks in your body, mind, and spirit of your energy system. As you do this work, notice shifts in your energy field; anxiety buffers down, and enthusiasm powers up using the potent mind-body tools, tapping, and other processes in *Your Playbook*. Use these tools and homeplay exercises often and in ways personalized to any situation.

These days, we can install a central command center in our homes. Each system—heat, air, water, electricity, and security—is monitored and controlled, often with a spoken command to a little box on the counter to complete a task. We can consider tapping as the master control that helps us focus on any part of our chakra system. Using this tool, we can tap into our thoughts, feelings, and emotions and have them flowing like central air, evenly cooling The House of You.

The transformations I have witnessed with my coaching clients continue to inspire me. And a higher purpose drives me to share this incredible process with as many women as possible. My client, Marie, demonstrates this opportunity to discover a new understanding of how and why we can get stuck.

Marie and the Porch Swing

"I don't know, Sandy. I'm so frustrated," said Marie. "I don't understand why I've been dragging my feet. I'm confounded by what should be a simple issue."

"Tell me a bit about that issue, Marie."

"We love living on the beach here in Nantucket, except the sea salt air and sand do a number on the house," Marie said, sounding dejected. "The furniture on the screened-in porch is old and tired. I love finding new pieces. However, I can't seem to spend money on a new porch swing. When I think about it, I get anxious. And all I do is think about it." Sounding resigned, Marie said, "Down deep, I think I have unresolved money issues."

I must tell you that I almost didn't accept Marie as a client. I knew I had a big task in front of me. She believed she was a lost cause, a total loser, and I was her last resort. Marie harbored intense anxiety about money. Even though she had plenty, she agonized about spending it, especially on a new porch swing. Along with her angst, Marie exhibited various symptoms of chakra blockage, including poor boundaries and feeling unworthy. She was stuck, unable to follow through on her dreams.

"Why am I so afraid? How can I get over this? I don't understand," Marie said. "And where's the joy? I thought things would be better by now." She paused. "I'm heartbroken because I realize that what I've lost is me." These words seemed to surprise her as if she discovered this truth as she spoke it.

Since she needed help to integrate this big aha moment, I took Marie through a process to calm herself that I learned from Margaret Lynch Raniere. After a few deep breaths, Marie came down from her busy mind and into her body. Then, I encouraged her to imagine a scan of her nervous system and visualize her stress lighting it up. "What's your daily average level of anxiety on a scale from zero to ten?" I asked.

"I'd say seven," Marie replied.

I looked into her eyes and said, "And you ramp up to ten at any given moment, right?"

Marie nodded. High anxiety was her habitual way of operating. She bit her fingernails to the quick to keep from screaming in panic or shouting in anger and rage.

Is Marie a ticking time bomb?

Before we could address anything else, she needed to feel safe in her body and secure in her home. I felt determined that we would shift the frenetic energy blocking her Root Chakra.

While tapping, we acknowledged and honored everything she'd been experiencing. This process helped her gain a new understanding of her hyper-vigilant, fight-or-flight stress response. Then, at the end of the tapping round, I asked her how she felt.

Marie's eyes grew wide. "While we were tapping, you said something that struck me. An old, vivid memory came up."

"What phrase was it, Marie?"

"There is no bear chasing me here in my house," she answered. She told me that when she was growing up in her large family in Louisiana, her mother relegated her to the screened-in porch to play during the day. She had to sleep out there, too, and her bed was the porch swing. Since she fit onto the swing cushion well, her mother said it was a perfect solution for a crowded house. "Except," Marie paused, "I was terrified out there."

I leaned in because we were getting somewhere. "How old were you then, Marie?"

"I was three," Marie said. "I had nightmares about a bear who lived under the porch. It would come out and chase me. I still smell the old, moldy, worn-out cushion." Marie's tense voice sounded like she was back there again. "I was so scared."

"Oh wow, what a frightening thing to go through," I said. "You were only three years old, alone on the screened-in porch and having nightmares." To help her inner child feel safe, I guided Marie through another round of tapping. Then, asking her to look at the image in her mind's eye again, I said, "Step into the picture as your adult self today. Put your arms around little Marie. Tell her she's safe now."

For the next step, I instructed Marie, saying, "Imagine a warm red light enveloping you both. Watch your little one shrink down and enter your heart, and as she nestles within you, give her your love."

We completed another round of tapping. Afterward, I asked her to rate her anxiety level again.

"It's down to three."

"That's awesome, Marie," I exclaimed. "You can see and feel how tapping works. Remember to tap whenever anxiety, fear, or other emotions and feelings come up."

Marie was calmer. Yet, she still spoke in a monotone, unexpressive, and deflated voice. We had more work to do. Money wasn't her only issue. Marie's 1st Chakra was blocked.

"I also had an aha moment today," I said. "You were three years old on that porch, alone in the dark and scared of a ravenous bear." Then, after pausing, I asked, "Do you notice that your terrifying trauma occurred on a porch swing? Might there be a connection to your fear about getting a new one?"

She shook her head in astonishment. "Oh my God, you're right. I repressed that memory. I knew that fear held me back for all these years. Yet I didn't know why."

"This step is one of many we're taking together, with me as your sacred witness. I hold the space for you to feel safe as we unravel unpleasant experiences. The processes are similar to your approach to interior design, Marie," I said. "You're turning your house into a home after years of putting it off."

As I write this account, I realize Marie's session was the first time I used the house renovation analogy.

We strengthen our core as we renovate our inner home. Like Marie, you have the right to reclaim your unique power, confidence, and beauty. You are safe. You've got this. And I've got you.

The Architect's Notes

Perhaps you're intrigued, as I was, by this unusual emotional healing method. Are you thinking about how tapping through your chakras to unblock the energy system within your body might work for you? The stories included in this book demonstrate that it's never too late. We don't have to stay stuck anymore.

Each of the seven major chakra energy centers contains long-held secrets to harnessing your inner power. The chakras also serve as storage rooms for memories. Our negative emotions wrap around the wounds and traumas of our past; many of us closed the rooms long ago. We locked the doors and forgot where we put the keys; sitting sentinel in the dark, our chakra shadows await our permission for release.

Ready to try unblocking your chakras with a tapping homeplay exercise? Let's start with something we all deal with at one point or another—stress. Go to Chapter Two of *Your Woo Woo Way Playbook* and practice Tapping for Stress.

In the next chapter, I share more about unblocking those shadows and why some ways you tried before might not have worked. Watch as energetic blocks clear in no time!

It wasn't until I started learning about the
chakra system (the body's seven energy centers)
that I felt the start of something big. As far as
I was concerned, I had suddenly found
a treasure map to healing.
—Margaret Lynch Raniere, *Unblocked*

The Architect's Notes
https://youtu.be/lv1VGwu_h4g

SCAN ME

Chapter Three

The House of You

https://youtu.be/POyibJ02GC4

The Elusive Bright Side

Spring 1999, Haircolor & Design Studio, Alexandria, Virginia

A tall, slender woman entered the salon, her bright sunny personality leading the way. "Hey, y'all," she said, flashing her signature big smile. She held out a large plate of fresh-baked yumminess and chirped, "How y'all doin'? I brought chocolate chip!"

This walking ray of sunshine was my old friend, Missy.

I swear. If we google-search happiness, a photo of Missy pops up. And she has a basket of goodies on her arm.

Everyone loved her, although sometimes we would all get weary of her over-the-top positivity.

However, something felt off when Missy sat down in my styling chair that day. I recognized telltale signs of unexpressed emotions hidden behind her smile. Shoulders slumped, she sighed at her reflection in the mirror. The sparkle was gone from her eyes. And dark circles under them spoke of tearful sleepless nights. Missy seemed a million miles away. My empathy grew because I saw a bit of myself in her. I knew how hard it was to hold a lid on inner turmoil. Like many women, Missy and I were taught, in no uncertain terms, to: "Always look on the bright side." Parents did not tolerate whining and complaining in the home, and sometimes such behavior was outright wrong.

Missy shared her life stories with me, feeling safe in what I called *the sanctity of the chair*. For instance, a teacher bullied her in front of everyone at school. Teachers were given full reign over us back then. Missy had felt humiliated, yet she never told her parents. She knew it would only bring further ridicule and punishment. Missy pushed her anguish down, vowing to stay quiet and appear happy while looking for the ever-elusive bright side.

In our circle of friends, she was always the positive one with kind, uplifting words. Even so, there were earlier times when I kept my distance from Missy. There was only so much pseudo-positivity I could take. It often wasn't what I needed. It wasn't Missy's fault. She lived in fear of being anything other than upbeat. And I knew something had to give. Eventually, Missy's inner emotional timebomb was going to explode.

The thing is, when something is wrong, blocking it from our minds doesn't work. Trying to pretend we're fine when we're upset makes the problem worse. With thoughts spinning in our heads, we get stuck in a loop of "toxic positivity."

Back in the salon that day, when Missy felt no one else could hear her, she grabbed my hand. Then, leaning in, she whispered, "I feel like I'm falling apart. My brain is foggy, and I'm an emotional wreck. I don't know what to do."

Fast Forward

Our lives have changed since those days in the salon. Missy's children are grown, she's divorced, and we're working together to unpack her past.

Throughout her life, Missy put her husband, children, and everyone else first. It's no wonder her health was failing. Her body, mind, and spirit took the toll of ignoring her feelings and needs.

"I kept waiting for it to be my time," she told me. "Now I'm freaking sixty years old, and I'm still stuck."

Missy now realizes why the wounds from her past never healed. She had swallowed, pushed down, and buried every sling and arrow that hurt her. Then, Missy pretended she was fine. But, of course, that's not even close to being fine.

When I started coaching her, Missy asked an important question. "I spent years reciting positive affirmations, hoping and praying for better outcomes. Why didn't they work?"

Affirmations *do* work. You know, like looking in the mirror and saying, "I am worthy" throughout the day. However, when we use affirmations, we may miss crucial steps. In addition to setting an intention for what we desire, we must imagine how we're going to *feel* when we get it. Perhaps that's happy, joyful, ecstatic, peaceful, free, or fulfilled. Embodying this higher vibrational feeling is the key to manifesting your wildest dreams.

Missy's affirmations never went anywhere because she couldn't feel what it would be like to be happy. Her blocked chakras restricted the flow of empowerment and manifestation energy. Meanwhile, Missy's faked joy had protected her when she needed it most. Through our sessions together, working through the chakras, she uncovered the hidden emotional blocks within her. Clearing them allowed her to feel safe enough to experience a full range of emotions. And tapping helped her deactivate her fears and anxiety.

I'm not saying it's wrong to look at the bright side—I practice and recommend it. However, we must observe the other, darker side to heal and grow in life. That's why each chapter about the chakras includes a whole section on the dark side, known as *the shadow*. Without addressing the shadow's negative energy, our affirmations won't work. And the source is often old traumas we must examine in our shadow selves to return to where we want to be, our authentic selves—balanced, happy, and at peace.

Why Affirmations Don't Always Work

There are books and programs galore on the law of attraction, manifestation, and abundance. However, I know dreams manifest faster when we go deep within to uncover the blocks in our 1st through 4th Chakras, the lower ones. They're the source of untapped hidden power. Nevertheless, positive thinking mandates encourage us to avoid thinking or saying anything negative—explaining that negativity only attracts more negativity. Instead, we must focus on the positive.

And yet, have you received disappointing results when you have attempted to practice positive affirmations? It can feel as if we're getting nowhere fast to look at a mirror and say over and over something we don't believe. Making little or no progress, we end up exhausted, frustrated, and stuck. We may ask ourselves, *What's wrong with me? I'm trying to be positive.*

The truth is—the dark, negative memories we've sidestepped still exist deep within us and sabotage those positive affirmations. The unexamined darkness continues to draw more destructive gunk our way. Buried and unexpressed negativity stifles our dreams, which is why our affirmations don't always work. Piled-up, unaddressed feelings and emotions clog our chakras, while the same behaviors and situations we tried to bury echo throughout our lives. An unattended physical injury won't heal. Likewise, until we voice and honor our internal wounds, they remain in our system, awaiting our attention to be healed.

When renovating our metaphorical house, a clogged drain can indicate yucky, built-up crud way down in the pipes. We must find the problem's origin, clear it with the proper tools, and allow water to flow again clearly and unobstructed. *Your Woo Woo Way Playbook* included in this book helps us uncover, clear, and heal the hidden emotional blocks obstructing the energy flow in our chakras using tapping, journaling, and meditation. There are also various more conventional approaches to seeking solutions to our problems, including prayer, meditation, yoga, crystals, candles, and essential oils. Most of us yearn for a connection to a Higher Power, so we love and need these spiritual practices. Hence, these methods focus on the upper chakras, 5th through 7th. When we bypass the lower chakras, frustration builds, and we stay stuck. Then, we feel as if our prayers go unanswered.

We often try to reach the stars from our rooftops before our inner foundation is solid enough to be built upon, and manifestation eludes us. To only focus on the upper chakras creates a struggle to access enlightenment. Once we unclog, clear, and heal the blocks in our lower chakras, we can go as far as we imagine.

At some point, holding all those bottled-up, unexpressed emotions becomes impossible. They burst out sideways when we least expect it. The emotional explosion resembles a frozen pipe. Pressure builds, the pipe breaks, and gushing water floods the basement. The outburst results in hurting others as well as ourselves. Angst, guilt, and regret wash over us. We hear from others how we've upset them, too. Then, without intervention and support, our emotional pain gets pushed back down again, and the cycle continues. Each additional traumatic experience piles on top of the rest, increasing pressure and making the foundation even less stable.

To manage the stress, we react with what's known as fight, flight, or freeze. A small, ancient part of the brain senses a threat and sends an intense energy charge through our bodies. With this natural reflex, we can react quickly in harmful situations. The charge dissipates when the imminent danger passes, and our bodies relax. However, with chronic stress from real or imagined danger, our minds and bodies remain on alert. Ever-present fear keeps us on edge, watchful for the next threat. Or we can calm the anxiety and stop the cycle. EFT tapping is the fastest way to shift our thinking and stop our stress-filled reactions.

Traumas

Let's look a little closer at those past hurts we carry. The spiritual mind-changing system, *A Course in Miracles,* tells us this maxim: "I am never upset for the reason I think." (ACIM, W-5) What on earth does that mean, *never?* When we're distressed, what we're upset about is all we think about, as we all know. We fixate on who or what to blame, and our thoughts spin out of control.

Meanwhile, according to our energy systems, how we respond feels the same as a past event. The echoes of old traumas, large or small, that develop in childhood stay hidden in the subconscious, where a part of us remains afraid and hyper-vigilant. And we wonder why we stay stuck, unable to move forward.

We experience different degrees of trauma throughout our lives. For example, "Big T" traumas, such as war and physical and sexual abuse, can and do destroy lives. However, while often overlooked, the "little t" traumas can be just as devastating for a third-grade child whose classmates ridiculed him for struggling with reading aloud. As a result, he may grow up into an adult terrified of public speaking. Or, in cases such as mine, we go silent, unable to speak up at all (more about this experience soon).

Our buried, denied, and often forgotten wounds cause repetitive behaviors to surface in every aspect of our lives. Then the behavior, such as not speaking up, becomes our go-to survival pattern throughout life. Yet "survival" doesn't mean the traumas go away. Instead, they stay with us, as Bessel van der Kolk, M.D., teaches in *The Body Keeps the Score*. The title of his New York Times bestselling book sums it up: Traumas build up within us and burrow in our bodies.

Over time, our overall health and well-being can diminish, and our entire existence crumbles like an old, neglected house. Those old traumas function like mold behind the walls or rust in the pipes. Then, we succumb to illnesses, injuries, diseases, and emotional instability.

In an upcoming chapter, I share a miraculous story of a coaching client whose metaphorical house was in disrepair when she first came to me. Now she's transformed—her restored house is a picture of health. Like her, we can all find our way through healing those traumas from our bodies, leading us back to our true, authentic selves, healthy and whole. We release our dis-ease and discomfort as we illuminate hidden, blocked energy. Our deep healing work on the chakra journey allows us to shine a light in the darkness.

Only The Shadow Knows

Our chakra journey includes illuminating the dark corners in our often-neglected virtual basements. It's bad enough to go into a dark, neglected basement in real life. To be asked to look inward here? You may think, *No, I don't want to go there. It's not safe. What if it's bad? I don't want to feel that.* We may feel like we're letting an untamed animal out of its cage.

Yes, investigating and poking around in the hidden parts of us is scary. After all, that is where we've stored and locked away the unacceptable stuff we don't want to admit we own. However, discovering and understanding our inner dark sides, the *shadow,* is crucial to the transformation journey. Our shadows, born of past wounds, hold the keys to unlocking the hold on us by our unwanted baggage.

While those shadows may be frightening, they're here to protect us. When they sense a threat, they trigger physical sensations in our bodies to get our attention. For example, our muscles may contract, and our hearts race. Or our chest tightens, making it hard to breathe. That's the shadow's early warning system to remind us about something that has hurt us before and may hurt us again.

Our shadows give us an aggravating bonus with our bodies' reactions—their unsolicited opinions. Have you been surprised when you considered trying something new, and all these fears and ideas came up with reasons for you not to proceed? Those voices come from your shadow. We often accept them as truth when we hear them, reinforcing self-doubt and unworthiness. Then, we beat ourselves up over our indecisiveness and inaction. There's usually a whole committee meeting in our heads without a seat at that table for us. This inner debate happens to all of us.

For example, you may get invited to a party and waffle on whether to attend. You think: *Part of me wants to go to the party. And another part wants to stay home, make popcorn, watch a movie, or maybe finish reading that book.* You can agonize over a simple decision until the last minute. Then, if you decide to attend the party, the thoughts continue to cascade: *What should I wear? Oh, I always wear that.* The shadow voices push and pull us to decide. *Oh, for crying out loud, pick something already.*

While a simple choice might be inconsequential, the brutal and degrading thought process can drive us mad when the moderator is our mean inner critic. That's your shadow, housing negative emotions such as fear, anxiety, guilt, grief, and shame.

These shadows have been with us even before birth. In the womb, we sense our mother's energy and emotions. From then, shadows take up residence in our bodies as our chakras develop through age twelve.

At a very young age, shadows help us make it in the world. Through trial and error, we identify ways to be cared for and stay safe. When we found what worked, those strategies became habits—like learning to be a "good and quiet" child. In time, these shadow-driven behaviors became our go-to survival patterns. When our lives felt threatened, we switched into survival mode, becoming prone to knee-jerk emotional reactions such as anger, neediness, people-pleasing, and self-sabotage. Sound familiar?

Consider how the shadow works when we're kids. In childhood, we often assumed that we'd be rewarded with love and attention if we were good. Some of us still feel that way. We can wear ourselves out doing good deeds for others and expecting affection in return. The thing is: *Sometimes positive attention wasn't available.* And studies have documented that negative attention is better than none. Since a neglected child does not thrive, our inner shadow protects us by earning attention. For example, by throwing a tantrum because we're tired and need a nap.

Our shadow is at work when we can get stressed out or triggered by the actions or words of others. We may react negatively with anger, tears, frustration, resentment, or resignation, or collapse into a helpless puddle. Others rant and fight back in rage. The scent of aftershave can trigger an unpleasant memory and make a woman freeze up in a panic. We often don't know why we have a specific reaction; however, the shadow's reaction time is immediate. We can use tapping to turn off this fight, flight, or freeze response automatically. Experience it yourself with the homeplay exercises in *Your Playbook*.

For all of us, at some point, our shadows arise. When we ignore our feelings coming from this inner part of us, the shadow doesn't give up. For example, if we push down a feeling of being overwhelmed, something more significant, such as fear, infects us—as when we ignore a nasty cut on our arm, and infection begins.

Now that you know how your shadow has been at work at times in your life that you'd love to do over, you might be surprised that my solution includes working *with* your shadows to feel better. Here's the key to understanding shadows: Shadows are within us because they love us and want to protect us when we need them most. That's their only job. These shadows have been a part of us throughout our whole lives. They helped us learn how to fight, freeze, or flee in our unique way to protect ourselves. Some of us may stay quiet and invisible, while others run from harm, or kick, scream, and fight like hell.

Whatever your shadow's go-to reaction, one of the most powerful steps we can take toward transformation is to accept our shadows. If we stuff our emotions down and "keep on keepin' on," another stronger feeling pops up. It's your shadow saying, "Oh, overwhelm and frustration aren't working. Send in FEAR, FEAR, FEAR." However, the secret to mastery is that when the shadows feel acknowledged, they turn into allies who help us conquer our deepest fears.

When it comes to the party invitation and how all the worries and self-doubt keep escalating, what if you changed course? When those questions about your outfit creep in, what if you tap and say, "Well, there you are, shadow. You're right. I do wear this dress a lot. Even though it's my favorite, I worry about wearing it again. What if they notice?" Then, once your shadow is acknowledged, it becomes an ally, accepting and valuing your favorite dress. The shadow lets go of its fear for your safety. Your anxiety calms, and you start changing the look by adding attractive accessories. Then you see yourself in the mirror and think, *I look fabulous in this dress. No wonder I love it. And I feel great in it.* The shadow of fear becomes your cheerleader, helping you feel confident at the party.

Even though our stuck negative energy doesn't go away, it no longer stays underground running the show. Instead, we transform it when we bring the shadow into the light and feel energized and empowered.

In these stories, lessons, and homeplay exercises, I share the way to self-empowerment by unblocking your chakras and harnessing their energy. During your homeplay, allow yourself to express all the hurts and injustices while analyzing past wounds. Then, unveil your shadows, the parts you hate or deny. Believe it or not, the negative emotions and behaviors we don't want to face have powerful gifts for us—often what we need the most.

Tapping, visualization, voice-dialoguing, and writing are techniques I use and teach to achieve transformation. For instance, with voice dialoguing, we converse with our shadows or write to them. They even write back. Then the shadow part of us feels heard and can let go of the fight, flight, or freeze. Other, more constructive responses become possible. EFT's founder, Gary Craig, says, "If it's bothersome, it's a tappable issue." Any time you need help, you can return to this book and *Your Playbook.*

In the next chapter, this beautiful work begins with the Root Chakra. First, we inspect for cracks in the foundation of The House of You so we can start to repair them.

By remaining stuck in the power of our wounds,
we block our own transformation. We overlook the greater gifts
inherent in our wounds—the strength to overcome them
and the lessons that we are meant to receive through them.
—Caroline Myss, *Why People Don't Heal and How They Can*

Chapter Four

The Foundation

The 1ˢᵗ Chakra Process

June 2017, Natick, Massachusetts
Intuitive Chakra Mastery Certification Workshop, Day 1
with Margaret Lynch Raniere

*W*hoa, wait a minute. No, no, not here. It's not how it's supposed to be. It's not the right place. It's so cold. Why are the walls putrid green? What's that funky smell? And what are those dreadful, shiny metal things and strange blinking, beeping machines? Who is this woman holding me by my tiny bottom in the palm of her big, beefy hand? Her uniform is starched so stiff I think it's going to crack. No wonder she looks so stern.

Trying to focus my newborn eyes, something feels off. My little arms pump and my legs kick hard and fast. Then, I push my heels out as if to hit the brakes midair.

This isn't right. Not these people. This is a horrible mistake. No, no, no.

The image was so clear it was palpable. Even though I couldn't recall my actual birth, I had a distinct *knowing*, something was off. It wasn't safe to be here. The cold hospital room gave me chills, and I almost gagged on the odor. Once outside my mother's womb, I felt the nurse smack my butt and clean me up. The first breath of air rushed in, stinging my lungs. When I was presented to my mom, I tried to scream with all my might. *Stop.* Yet all I could muster was a mournful, fearful cry.

Searching the delivery room, I wondered if anyone else was there.

Where's my father? He's not here. Why isn't he here? Where's my dad?

My adult brain knew that in 1949, dads were often not present for a child's birth. However, my inner little one wanted me to see this.

Where's Daddy? Maybe he's at work? I guess that's normal. Or he could be at Red's Bar drinking his paycheck again.

For my dad, that's normal too.

I witnessed my newborn self stepping into the foundation of my new, metaphorical home. The 1st Chakra energy center formed in my physical body. I was already taking in my family's circumstances, environment, and inherent belief system. A soon-to-be familiar phrase echoed in my mind, becoming an unquestioned truth. "People like us," it said. Then, it followed with, "We can't, we don't, we won't ever, we never ___." Fill in the blank. All these worries and restrictions that constantly threatened my safety blocked my Root Chakra. Cracks continued to form in my virtual foundation, stunting my emotional growth.

Do I Belong Here?

The 1st Chakra is our foundation of safety and belonging in the world. At birth, our tiny nervous systems experience fear and uncertainty. Even with ideal parents and caregivers, there can be frightening moments. For instance, we cry out when hungry or when our tush is wet and soiled. We wail for the warmth of human touch and a soothing, reassuring voice.

The situation can be less than perfect. Yet, we find ways to adapt and survive when soft voices and comfort don't arrive. Either way, we burst into reality at birth. Confused and scared, we face these foundational questions that I uncovered in the 1st Chakra Visualization in the story that opens this chapter:

Am I safe here?

Do I belong here with this family?

Does anybody care that I'm here?

Do I want to stay here?

How do I live?

Do I deserve to be loved?

The way we answer these questions in infancy correlates to the development (or lack thereof) of our Root Chakra. Therefore, it's crucial to shine a light in the dark corners of our virtual basements. We begin with the 1st Chakra to uncover the root causes of our problems in adulthood, renovating, refurbishing, and strengthening the foundation.

Empowerment energy starts to flow through the 1st Chakra. When it's blocked, we can't reach our potential. Therefore, we must reclaim our birthright power and energy by unblocking the early shadows formed to protect our baby selves.

If you've always had your basic needs met, it's easy to presume that your entry into this world was warm and loving. And perhaps you received affection from devoted parents or caregivers. Nevertheless, you may still be dealing with anxiety, fear, uncertainty, and a host of other emotions stemming from your birth. And if you already know you had a challenging start in life, you may carry hurt feelings from those events. These shadows become chronic stresses that indicate weak underpinnings in your inner virtual home if left unhealed.

The last step of my birth visualization process was to let my baby self shrink into my heart. Then, I gave her the love and protection she needed. When I opened my eyes, I realized I was rocking myself in a slow, rhythmic motion. I felt safe, with my inner baby wrapped in self-love, perhaps for the first time.

Wow, that's interesting. I guess I needed to rock myself.

A solid, revitalized foundation gives us the love we need and deserve— the love that's been missing. You can start now to patch the cracks. Take a breath, envision your inner child, and give your love to her. She's waiting for you. She needs you.

Crumbling Foundation – Blocked Root Chakra
Disempowering, negative impact: fear, anxiety, terror

The 1st Chakra includes our physical body and everything solid around us. It's the chair we sit on at home, the office, or school. The Root Chakra is the foundation that sets the groundwork for everything above it. We feel unsupported and unsafe when this chakra is weak or blocked.

When nurtured and loved, this positive energy from the caretakers or parents paves the way for a baby to reflect an open 1st Chakra. However, some infants don't receive the love and care they need when the energetic circuit between them and their parents does not exist.

Their 1st Chakra is blocked. The fears and negative beliefs of their parents infiltrate their inner being. And then, these disconnected babies become dissociated adults.

A blocked 1st Chakra can trap us in a dizzying array of thoughts. As a result, solutions to problems remain elusive. Without solid footing, we're uncomfortable sensing the feelings and emotions our bodies send us. We think it's better to avoid feelings altogether and instead utilize our brains. Therefore, we're unaware of our bodies and how much they can tell us. Instead, we fixate only on thoughts for days, months, or even years.

When a client says, "I don't think I feel anything," I know she's denying and rejecting her body and operate from her head. The 1st Chakra is about safety. She needs to be grounded and feel safe enough to accept her feelings as a part of her. Then, as she uncovers and clears her blocked emotions, she can repair her inner power grid.

With a blocked Root Chakra, daily stressors cause our thoughts to spin. Anxiety and worry escalate. We're not grounded or present in our bodies when we are overwhelmed with all those concerns. Therefore, our physical and emotional safety and security are always in question. Have you known anyone who seemed only to feel safe when anxious? For them, stress regularly impacts every part of their lives. They have trouble sleeping from hyper-vigilance (clenched jaw) and recurring worries. As a result, they can't relax even in their sleep.

We may survive by using brainpower and being amped up on stress. Yet, do we thrive? What happens when we lose ourselves in thought, engrossed in studies or daydreams? Without a grounded, solid Root Chakra, we're frightened of the world. This fear drives a compulsion to research on the internet for every ache and pain. We're sure it's the worst possible scenario. It's also difficult to let anyone get close to us when we stay inside our heads, oblivious to them. An exaggerated example of a person with a blocked 1st Chakra is Sheldon Cooper, the lead character in the television series, *The Big Bang Theory*. He's an overly intellectual nerd with a general lack of humility, empathy, and social skills. And he's frightened of virtually everything.

Adults with Root Chakra blockage can seem aloof. They feel safest and most comfortable using their intellect. Mentally absent, they're often oblivious to what's going on around them. And other people don't notice them either. They may say, "Oh, I didn't see you there. Have you been here the whole time?"

Solid Foundation – Open, Unblocked 1st Chakra
Empowering, positive effect: safe, grounded, solid presence

With free-flowing energy in the 1st Chakra, we're rooted, down to earth, and secure. There's a solid sense of safety and belonging with a drive to live in the now. Remaining present in our bodies, not distracted in our minds, we feel our emotions as they arise. Being focused and grounded connects us to ourselves and others. If we pull our heads out of the clouds, our thoughts and ideas come to fruition. Sounds good, right?

The first step to solidifying our foundation is noticing when and how often we're anxious. Then, we can begin to catch ourselves in the middle of repetitive worrisome thoughts. *Yes, those thoughts.* We're full of them. Has this ever happened to you? First, you're thinking about one thing, and your mind runs off in another direction. Then, you get caught in thought, ruminating about the past or fretting about the future.

This next story demonstrates how awareness initiates healing.

In the thick of it – Pandemic Panic
New York City, New York, 2020

"I need your help, Sandy," said Lara, a new referral. Her brilliant, cobalt blue eyes spoke of intense anxiety, fear, and sorrow—typical signs of a blocked 1st Chakra. Even in the Zoom frame, I saw visible tension in her body and pain pinched on her face. Her thin hair hung in string-like strands on her shoulders. Gaps were exposing her scalp. The former hairdresser in me recognized how excess shedding results from chronic stress. Hair is an excellent barometer for what's going on in our bodies.

"I'm an emergency room physician here in New York City," Lara said, speaking in rapid, staccato bursts of anxious worry coupled with exhaustion. Her eyes widened and her voice crackled with palpable dread. "The hospital is overrun with COVID patients. The mortality rate is climbing. They've hijacked every available space for patients and hospital staff erected tents in the parking lot. We're overburdened and overwhelmed attempting to keep patient after patient alive."

I leaned forward and nodded, not wanting to interrupt. An emotional dam was about to break.

"My hair keeps falling out and I can't afford to lose any more. Look, my scalp is showing. We don't have time to eat. I can't sleep. I've tried everything, barring medications. Nothing works." She looked at me with those sorrowful, pleading eyes and said, "I know that you use EFT. Would you do some tapping with me today?"

"Take a breath for a moment. I've got you," I said. "You're right, Lara. Tapping is a tool I use and teach in my coaching practice. It's not part of my initial discovery calls. However, I see your stress. I assure you, I won't let you go until we bring your anxiety level down. I promise to guide you through a tapping session at the end of our conversation. How does that sound?"

She nodded her head and sighed in agreement. Her speech slowed a bit as she told me her story. "Even though I've dealt with anxiety my whole life, this crisis has me on edge."

My hand went to my heart. "Oh Lara, I'm so sorry for your suffering. That's so much to endure."

Because her 1st Chakra was blocked, Lara had no ground to stand on. She kept trying to use her brain to break out of the prison of her anxious thoughts. And immersed in her busy schedule, Lara wouldn't take the time to focus on feeling emotions stored in her body. As a result, she remained overwhelmed, on the verge of panic.

Lara was looking in the wrong places. She visited the hospital chapel for silent reflection and practiced intermittent yoga. Both helped calm her mind; however, the effects didn't last. Lara's clogged Root Chakra allowed only a trickle of energy to travel upward through her chakra system. Bypassing her emotions, she pushed them down and soldiered on, behaving like a good girl trying to stay out of trouble.

Lara also had long-standing issues with her father. "I don't know why I'm thinking more about him lately. He's judgmental, mean, and angry. I'm a doctor, for crying out loud. According to him, though, I can't do anything right. He criticizes everything I do or say, so I'm always trying to prove myself to him."

The pandemic stress had triggered old traumas with her father.

"Lara, tell me your goals," I said. "Paint me a picture of your perfect, average day. Not the one where you win the lottery. Your ideal day-to-day life. Describe it."

"Right now," Lara said, "all I care about is calming my nerves and getting healthy again. I want peace. I want joy." She took another breath, then sighed. "And down the road, I'd like to be in a loving relationship." A tiny glimmer of hope flickered in her eyes.

I asked Lara to rate her anxiety, and she immediately responded. "Oh, no question, it's the maximum ten plus." We talked through where she felt discomfort in her body. She felt tightness in her neck and shoulders, a pounding headache, and low back pain. These signs indicated a blocked 1st Chakra, the seat of fear and anxiety. As Lara would escape into her head and keep her feelings to herself, the aches and pains in her upper body stemmed from trying to hold it all in. Did you know that we store emotions in our organs? Fear settles in the kidneys, which sit in our lower backs. I needed to help Lara get grounded, feel safe, and release some physical and emotional pain.

Finally, following our initial exchange, I led her through a round of tapping. Lara voiced her pain and all the negative, menacing, swirling thoughts in her head—the unfairness, worry, angst, and sadness—spilled out of her. Then, she exhaled a long sigh, and her shoulders dropped, signaling an energy shift. We finished with a round of calming affirmations.

"How do you feel now, Lara?"

"Oh my God, I feel so much better."

"How about your physical pain?"

"The tension is gone from my neck and shoulders. My heartbeat seems slower, and my back doesn't hurt as much."

"You were at ten plus when we started. What's that number now?"

She responded with incredulity. "It's down to one. I'm relaxed and relieved. It's like a miracle." Lara was elated and might have jumped out of her chair if she weren't so relaxed.

"That's incredible," I said. "Coming down even one or two points is huge. Notice the difference. Trapped energy causes constriction in your body. That overall tension makes it hard to function or think clearly. And, any time you feel this way again, you can use tapping to relax your body and clear your mind."

In the coming months, I guided Lara on an inner journey to uncover, clear, and heal her past traumas. At a young age, Lara learned to run and hide to avoid her father's anger and criticism, establishing her survival pattern of mental and physical escape. Believing she was unworthy, this accomplished doctor spent her life striving to prove herself. She used logic and pragmatism, becoming more robotic. Resisting her feelings, Lara would drift off and escape into her mind. Inside the safe container of our coaching sessions, she faced these long-buried wounds of her past where she had locked away many memories and emotions.

In an early session, Lara met her inner child and created a safe space for her to be vulnerable. To begin, the inner Little Lara expressed her wants and needs for love and attention. Then, on the next call, she voiced her feelings of fear, pain, rejection, abandonment, and anger. Once this part of her felt heard and acknowledged, Lara accepted the gifts her shadow held. They were the very gifts she needed most, safety and security anchored in self-compassion and love.

Over time, Lara felt safe enough to shine a light in the dark parts of her chakras. She was glowing with health and vitality from her experience of this magical transformation in body, mind, and spirit. The last time I spoke with Lara, she radiated love and enthusiasm. Once she started to shift her energy, other people changed, and her work stresses evaporated. Every aspect of her life turned around. She didn't dwell on blame, regret, sadness, or fretting about the future.

And my inner hairstylist was thrilled because Lara's hair was thicker, full of body and shine. In the salon, I often witnessed how creating external changes for women affected their internal character. In a similar way, an internal transformation changes our outer appearance.

"You won't believe what's happened," Lara said. "It's wild. My hair is growing back in, and I get compliments all the time. I'm more balanced and not anxious. I'm stronger than I've been in a long time. I'm so grateful I found you—and tapping."

As Lara's strength grew, she set healthy boundaries. Even her father's intense criticism waned. He relaxed his need to control her and expressed immense pride in his daughter. She didn't feel friction with him anymore. Moreover, her new, empowered presence brought compliments from her superiors, coworkers, and family.

Today Lara is thriving, no longer stuck and overwhelmed. Her inner energy is flowing upward and outward. She feels safe in her body and doesn't have to retreat into her mind anymore.

Shadow Power – From Fear to Safety and Security

Some part of us disagrees when setting a goal, or even contemplating one. A debate unfolds, and confusion sets in. For example, while part of you may have a goal to buy and restore an old Victorian house, another part worries about the struggle to pay the mortgage and all the renovation costs. A different part fears that the property's value could plummet, and your investment may tank. And yet another aspect of you only thinks about termites, rotting wood, and tree roots breaking through the foundation.

This internal argument happens whether we're setting a goal to exercise every day, get more sleep, change careers, or enjoy a long-term love relationship. As we monitor the dueling fears, we hear familiar phrases like, "It takes too much effort," "You can stay up for one more episode," "Play it safe," "Stay where you are," "You're not good enough," and "You're too old." Too often, we end up in a stalemate with those conflicting fears, unable to move forward.

When we need to make a decision, we often spend time ruminating with the committee inside our heads. It's common to consult our brains to find a way out of difficulty. Or we may approach a concern with tools from the spiritual realm like prayer, meditation, candles, essential oils, yoga, or reiki. We love these practices and need them to engage our upper chakras. However, our energy can't flow like that from top to bottom when we've got shadow blockages in the lower chakras. *Yep, you guessed it.* The shadows are the parts of us we keep pushing down and trying to deny.

For Lara, the Root Chakra shadow of fear ruled her anxiety-driven actions. This ever-fearful part caused her to dissociate and disconnect from her body. She thought dilemmas would clear if only she would put her mind to them.

Like Lara experienced, the energy locked inside our negative emotions can be released and accelerate our transformational journey. It may sound scary. Nonetheless, when we come down into our bodies, we allow ourselves to feel, perhaps for the first time. As you unblock old fears, you make room for safety and security.

One of the fastest, most effective ways to unblock fear is tapping. And adding guided visualization during tapping brings new perspectives to build safety and security. Then we see how our realities and belief systems formed early in life. Facing our shadows, we learn how parental figures, teachers, and religious, political, and cultural leaders influenced our lives.

Many lessons planted limiting beliefs in us early in the 1st Chakra stage of development. Then, as the other chakras develop throughout childhood, they sit upon this foundation of perceived truth formed by repetitive limiting thoughts. For example, "I'm not good enough" or "Good girls don't speak up" trigger fear when we even think of standing up for ourselves as adults. Limiting beliefs may also evolve from reprimands. Mom said, "Don't touch the hot stove," which only piqued our curiosity. Then, when we got burned, we believed it was because we were bad. These limiting beliefs about being bad gave birth to fear, our shadow. While it sounds convoluted, our shadow loves us and only wants to protect us. It doesn't believe we are bad; it's just worried about us getting burned and punished again. The shadow watches out for the hot stove moments to keep us safe and triggers us into fight, flight, or freeze.

The shadow reacts when it perceives a threat. Rising fear causes our bodies to constrict. Our minds spin, and our empowerment energy is blocked, stifling our manifestation power. Then we're stuck instead of being able to create the best possible outcome.

Get ready. Here's the woo woo part. We can talk to our shadows to change our reactions. While tapping, the conversation allows each shadow (guilt, anger, shame, sadness) to feel heard and acknowledged. They come out of the dark and into the light, no longer needing to hide. As a result, our energy shifts, and we feel released from fear, freeing ourselves from whatever in the past holds us back.

Not sure which shadow to talk to first? They speak to you all the time by sending signals. They show up as feelings, emotions, and bodily sensations. For example, we might feel anxious, or have a headache, queasy stomach, shortness of breath, and other symptoms. Unfortunately, many of us tend to ignore these signs, escaping straight into our thoughts. And sometimes, the shadow sends a subtle undercurrent of a general feeling that something's not right. Next time that happens, you're able to start an inner dialogue.

By paying attention to our bodies, we can feel the sensations before a stressful thought enters our minds. Tapping on the symptoms we feel in the body calms our nervous system, telling the shadows that we're safe and it's okay to relax.

Whenever we inquire deeply enough into the truth about our suffering, we arrive at a place where, without changing direction, we stop descending and start ascending.
—Martha Beck, *The Way of Integrity*

Message from the Foundation

I AM your foundation of strength, the 1ˢᵗ Chakra. I cement your right to safety, security, and resilience.

When I'm blocked, I stop your system's natural flow of empowerment energy. Then, you may resort to problematic thinking, anxiousness, and hyper-vigilance. Staying invisible and avoiding crowded situations becomes your go-to survival pattern.

You may not seem to feel fear at all. You may appear to be in total control and always need to be in control. You keep your negative emotions at bay, becoming quite disturbed if anything goes wrong. Or, you may be hyper-vigilant and anxious with one emergency after another—seemingly with no end. You may be an over-talker. You want to share all your ideas, strategies, and everything in your head, taking over conversations to avoid troublesome issues in your foundation.

Clearing the blocks hidden in me, your Root Chakra, allows you to pour a solid foundation for your inner home. Then, you can stand with your feet firmly planted, claiming your right to be here on this planet. When grounded in safety, you are meeting your physical and emotional needs. With me open, empowerment energy rises to meet the chakras above, starting with the 2ⁿᵈ Chakra. Your journey of self-empowerment, transformation, and manifestation has begun.

Check out Chapter Four of *Your Playbook* to start 1ˢᵗ Chakra clearing. Of course, the more you practice, the more clearing you do. The Tapping for Anxiety is less than two minutes, and I show you exactly how to customize your tapping session.

In the next chapter, see what happens as the energy you released from the 1ˢᵗ Chakra rises to fuel your 2ⁿᵈ Chakra.

1ˢᵗ Chakra, Message from the Foundation
https://youtu.be/eAHluDmClnQ

Chapter Five

The Basement

The 2nd Chakra – Me, My Husband, and God

July 2017, Savannah, Georgia

"Good damn you, Dennis. You never got a hold of yourself," I yelled. "You blamed everyone else other than you. You refused to get help. You stewed in anger! You wallowed in regret! You were stuck in self-pity! You thought you could numb your pain and blot out the world with alcohol and drugs. It didn't work, did it?"

I was alone, shouting and tapping the side of my hand against the steering wheel of my blue Toyota Yaris, Little Blue Jellybean. I was on a five-minute drive to the natural foods grocery store, my only alone time as the around-the-clock caretaker for Dennis.

"I hate you for how you did this to yourself, and how you treated me. I'm so disappointed in you, in us." My voice grew louder and stronger as I felt my anger rise from somewhere deep inside of me.

Cautionary note: Tapping in your car while driving is dangerous. It's advisable to park where you feel safe to express your emotions while tapping.

The previous day, I shared with my coach that my husband's dementia was worsening. His heart disease had advanced as well.

She asked, "Sandy, have you done anger tapping?"

"Yes, a little. It's hard to find time alone, though. And the apartment walls are too thin."

"It's important for you to do the anger work. Or you may have a more challenging time grieving when Dennis dies," she said. "You can do it in your car and get loud. I promise you won't be sorry. I want you to do it as if it's a three-way conversation. Start by picturing your husband in front of you. Tell him about all the pain and sorrow you've felt over all these years. Second, voice the anger toward yourself and how you never felt strong enough to confront him."

She encouraged me to yell and scream about my inability to change him, make him get help, or get help for myself. Then, she leaned forward and said, "Part three, express your anger at God."

My jaw dropped in shock. She was my coach and also a minister.

"God?" I asked, dumbfounded. "What about free will? Isn't that the whole idea? I'm suffering the consequences of my own choices, right?"

She gave me a compassionate smile. "No. You asked for help, and you didn't get it."

I sat there silent for a moment. Kimberly had no way of knowing I'd begged God and the Holy Universe for help. I'd already done so much of what I called pre-grieving, both preparing for his death and mourning the loss of what could have been. However, she helped me get through so much. I committed to trying the anger-tapping conversation process; I was willing, even though I wasn't sure it would do any good.

A few days later, I found an opportune time to try anger tapping. I was able to leave Dennis for a short time in the mornings. I hopped into my Little Blue Jellybean and drove off. At first, when I tapped the steering wheel, I was only pretending to be mad. Like many women, my upbringing taught me never to get angry. It's not appropriate. It's not a good look; stay quiet and sweet. I knew I loaded my life with be-a-good-girl strategies.

Tapping the steering wheel, I whispered, "I'm not angry. I'm just disappointed. I'm frustrated. Maybe I'm mad." Then I started to raise my voice, louder and louder, angrier and angrier. As I stopped for the red light at the second intersection, I was yelling and tapping on my face and collarbone. At last, I screamed, "Damn you, Dennis."

Then I became aware of a police car on my right. A woman and three children were in a sedan to my left.

They must think I'm a crazy woman. It's too late now. I'm in full-blown anger mode. I'm not stopping.

Both cars turned onto different roads, and I continued straight ahead. *Phew.* I kept tapping and switched to focus the anger on me.

"I'm so mad at you, Sandy. You're so weak. You endured so much. Yet you kept taking it anyway. You figured out Dennis had PTSD, and still, you did nothing. Oh yeah, even though you learned all about it, you were too scared to talk with him or suggest he seek treatment. You thought he'd get even angrier if you broached the subject. You were afraid of losing him. Now you've lost him anyway. Why couldn't you step up? Things could be so different now. You're pathetic," I yelled, choking on tears.

At the next light, I turned right onto a tree-lined street. A canopy of Spanish moss dangled from the Southern Live Oak trees arched over the road. It gave the space a reverence, Mother Nature's cathedral.

It's not right to raise your voice in church. You should never speak the name of the Lord in vain.

The Catholic girl in my head had no chance. I yelled as loud as I could. I'd never screamed that loud before, nor since.

I shrieked, "This is on you, God. I blame you. How could you allow this to happen? Why didn't you help me? I begged and pleaded for relief, day after day, night after night. I'm so tired and so very sad. What kind of test are you giving me? It's not fair."

At this point, I reached the angry cry. Something shifted in me. Continuing to tap the steering wheel, I acknowledged my pain. "I'm just going to honor how I feel. I'm exhausted and tired of all of this. I honor that I've been through a lot. I'm drained, and I still need to keep going. I honor all of it."

Pulling into the store's parking lot, I parked my car and turned off the engine. I couldn't get out of the car, though. Something incredible was happening. My arms seemed to float up and out. I felt a sensation of electric energy, a bolt of white lightning moving through my body. I sat there with my arms in the air.

Wow, this is interesting.

I released a massive amount of trapped energy in about seven minutes.

Returning home, I felt a decisive shift within me. Far more patient, I found it easier to see Dennis as the young, innocent child that dementia had made of him. I acknowledged, voiced, honored, and moved the energy it took to hold onto years of buried anger, disappointment, and frustration. My husband's energy also shifted after I vented that verbal diatribe. Therefore, we had less tension and friction, and Dennis was less frustrated and calmer.

With empowerment energy flowing through me, I held steadfast during the next and final stage of my husband's decline. His diagnosis of six months or less had lasted four years. During that time, I often cried, pre-grieving. Nevertheless, no amount of tears accomplished what this anger tapping did for me. Even when my clients don't think they have anger, I take them through an anger release process, and the anger shadow feels safe enough to come out and be heard.

The Basement – Life Force Energy

When a block in the 1st Chakra is released, a spark of safety ignites the fuel in the Sacral (2nd) Chakra, the seat of our deepest desires. Many people assume the 2nd Chakra is all about sex and sexuality. However, it's much more. The Sacral Chakra stores life force energy, our power source for creativity, prosperity, and passion. In the virtual house renovation project, the basement is our hub for this power. The primary electrical circuits, water heater, furnace, and air conditioner live here. Everything must run at optimum performance and efficiency. If the power goes out, we need a flashlight to avoid stumbling in the dark. Here on The Woo Woo Way journey, we shine a light inward on the 2nd Chakra.

The Sacral Chakra reflects the very definition of duality. Delivered with every negative aspect is a glowing, positive gift if we choose to open it. It can be hard to see the gift in anger, for instance. We don't like anger of any kind. However, on the other side of anger is passion. And the energy of passion drives our creative endeavors, intentions, dreams, goals, and adventures.

Instead of choosing, we can embrace the concept of both aspects of each emotion expressed in the 2nd Chakra. For example, when asking for what we want, others might perceive us as selfish. Yet the gift behind selfishness is vulnerability. In other words, we can be both needy and generous. *I'm not a needy person, but I have a needy side. And I'm kind and giving.* It is challenging for many women to ask for what we need and want, yet our lives dramatically change when we do.

Boxes in the Basement – Blocked 2nd Chakra
Disempowering, negative impact:
self-rejection, repressed anger, frustration

When we move into a house, we often overload the basement with excess stuff. And we shlep it with us through every move. It's the same with our 2nd Chakra. Our disappointments and resentments, plus our wants, needs, and desires, are stashed and then locked in the basement closet. We throw away the key and forget they even exist. As a result, we block the on-fire energy of the Sacral Chakra. And unboxing years of stored negative energy can seem like too much work. Nevertheless, when we decide to locate the key, we can reclaim our deepest desires.

Beginning in childhood, we look to our authority figures for acceptance, validation, reassurance, and a sense of belonging. We take in the world around us with sensual joy and vitality. Then, if we don't get love and appreciation, we become acceptable to our family and community standards by molding ourselves into someone else. And we cram our virtual basement with boxes stuffed with unfulfilled dreams.

When our natural urges and desires get squashed, our emotions awaken, begging for us to notice them. If blocked, we learn at a young age that asking for what we want or need is not safe. Many of us grew up with stereotypical gender restrictions. It could be as simple as boys being allowed to go outside and play. The girls, meanwhile, had to stay in to help their mothers get dinner on the table. Sometimes there were tears. However, we quickly wiped them away because we got the message: To get parental approval, we had to behave and be good girls. Boys can be boisterous. Girls must be ladylike. Discouraged, we stopped asking. Then we packed our wishes and disappointments away.

The impact of our unexpressed emotions doesn't go away. They remain inside us, waiting to be released when it feels safe, although keeping them hidden can feel safer. It's often too much to bear, yet too much to unburden. That's how the letdowns, heartbreaks, and other negative emotional wounds pile up as life progresses.

What rules did you learn as a child? What were you told to be—or not to be? For example, parents often caution children not to be too weak or too emotional. Nor should we be too full of ourselves or too loud. Or, as my mom would say, "Don't get too big for your britches." Fear of breaking these rules blocks our powerful Sacral Chakra. By restricting our feelings, we deny our inner power and passion. Ultimately, we think we're unworthy of our desires, not good enough, or unlovable if we ask for or go after what we really want.

As I said before, many of us, including me, take on the persona of the good little girl. We're models of good behavior, staying safe and away from verbal or physical harm. We play small and keep quiet into adulthood, not daring to make any waves. We stop wanting anything important to us, flying under the radar of the "behavior police." Fearful of confrontation and retribution, I tried hard not to be angry at my husband, Dennis. For example, I could never broach the subject of his drug and alcohol addiction.

Our bodies pay the price when our energy stays blocked by a stockpile of emotional wounds. Muscles constrict, and joints and vital organs weaken. Often, we succumb to illness or disease. Or we're susceptible to accidents, broken bones, skin problems, or hair loss.

Our voices and dreams get suppressed, and our silenced longings fester. We can't conceive of having a carefree moment with this shutdown energy.

On the other hand, we might also become the girl who spends her life trying to prove her worth. It's not enough to just be good at what we do. We must be excellent. Our inner taskmaster drives us toward achievement and top performance. The epitome of the overachieving woman, we yearn for acceptance and approval. And simmering unexpressed frustration, anger, and anxiety hovers behind our smiles. A blocked 2nd Chakra causes us to resist achieving our true goals and dreams. We live in dread of shame and continue punishing ourselves with extended hours.

If you see yourself as trying to be a "good girl," you might describe trying to step out of your comfort zone in one or more of these phrases: *I can't, I shouldn't, I'm too afraid to do that,* or *It's shameful.* That day when I screamed, ranted, and raved in the car, I allowed my good little girl to have a tantrum, the one she'd never dared have till then.

Those who strive to prove their worth may look at challenges and say, "I have to. If I don't do it, I'd be mortified." On the other hand, you might already be more than enough, and you don't have to keep proving yourself. I think of Serena Williams, a world-class tennis player who chose to retire to make room for other priorities in her life. No more championships to defend her titles. I'm heartened by young women today. Whether athletes or scholars, they pull themselves out of stressful, competitive situations when their physical or mental health is in jeopardy. Let's learn from their examples.

To unblock our chakras, we look at our whole selves, our light, and our dark. During the coaching process, we peek into the dark, shining light on everything we left behind. That's how we reclaim our true selves. The dark part of us no longer needs to stay in the shadows, not even the anger or the guilt we carry because of it.

Unpacked Basement – Unblocked 2nd Chakra
Empowering, positive effect: desire, feeling valued, creative, passionate

To paraphrase Cheryl Strayed in her book, *Tiny Beautiful Things*, we must find a place to put our negative feelings. If we don't, they rule us. We begin to see their value when we can accept the negative parts of us that we tried to deny. There's a beautiful gift on the other side of our anger. However, we're often afraid to express it. Nonetheless, we need the energy of passion, including anger, to bring our dreams and vision into reality.

The on-fire energy in our 2nd Chakra holds the fuel to power us into action in the 3rd chakra. A blast of energy is released when we allow all our long-forgotten, rejected, and deepest needs to be voiced and acknowledged. Using EFT tapping, the released energy ignites our inner power in a way that proves our fears unfounded. No one gets hurt, not even us.

As little children, our deepest needs were simple. We wanted love, acceptance, and attention. Yet, we often didn't feel safe enough to dare ask for them. However, we can use visualization processes to reconnect with our inner child and her unfulfilled desires. For example, she gets to tell her parents how they failed her. When she says everything she couldn't say before, this freedom to express herself unblocks her Sacral Chakra.

You give your younger self permission to say, "I want you to see me, hear me, love me. I want to feel special and adored." These are the very same needs we crave today, right? When you respond to your inner child's needs, as I did with my infant self, you heal and are empowered to move forward.

Annie – 911 Call

A familiar chord chimed. With the reflex of Pavlov's dogs, I picked up my phone. "HELP," began the text from Annie. She wrote, "Do you have time for a 911 call? I'm in a lot of pain and can't seem to alleviate it."

I responded without hesitation. "Of course, call me now."

My private VIP clients receive bonus "911" calls. Anytime between our bi-monthly sessions, they can request a quick tapping call. We usually work on a specific issue, trigger, or pain that has come up for them.

"I didn't want to disturb you, but this is bad," Annie said. "I'm beside myself trying to lessen this pain."

I felt her depleting energy and heard the ache in her voice.

"I shoveled heavy snow yesterday. Today, the pain in my hip is excruciating. It radiates down my leg to my knee and ankle. And now it's moved into my lower back. Nothing I try is giving me any relief."

"No worries, Annie. I'm happy to help," I replied. "We can tap on the pain."

"We just worked on the 1st and 2nd Chakras. Could this be connected?" Annie asked.

"Absolutely," I exclaimed. "Let's address the emotions trapped in your hip and the pain you're feeling."

I asked Annie to tell me what thoughts were running through her head. Then, I led her through a short tapping round. Repeating after me, she tapped and said, "I'm in so much pain; it hurts so bad. I feel it in my back and my leg. Everything hurts."

We switched to probable emotions, and she repeated my questions as she continued to tap. "Is this fear?" "What am I afraid of?" "Or maybe I'm mad." "Is this anger?" "What am I angry about?"

Afterward, I had her pause to take a deep breath.

"Did anything come up for you?" I asked.

"Oh yeah, big time, 1986," Annie shouted.

"Whoa, Annie, what happened in 1986?"

She told me about a skiing accident. "It started when I was going too fast and moved to the other side of the slope to slow down. Then I tumbled headfirst into an unmarked hole. The right ski boot released, and the left ski boot didn't. I hung upside down, terrified, screaming for help. There was considerable damage and breakage to my left foot, ankle, knee, and—" she paused. "Hip."

"Oh, wow, Annie, how frightening."

"It was. That's not all, though," Annie declared in dismay. "My so-called friend who was skiing with me just kept going. She left me there and never looked back, never sent help."

Indeed, her emotional response indicated residual anger surfacing that I knew I could help her release with tapping.

I fed Annie over-the-top, vengeful, tapping statements. And she screamed, "How dare you leave me." "I am so f-ing mad." "You left me there." "I could've died." "I couldn't get out." "I'm so angry." "You never even checked on me." "I could've severed my spine or broken my neck." "What a horrible excuse for a human being you are." On we tapped and ranted. Annie spewed all the anger and rage she'd buried from this long-forgotten incident.

Then I switched to tapping with calming affirmations. As she tapped, Annie said, "I'm open to releasing this pain." "I'm open to letting go of the anger and bringing down the pain." "Relaxing the pain now." "Feeling relief now."

"How do you feel now, Annie?" I asked.

"Sandy, there's no pain. Wow, no pain at all," she said, beginning to cry. "Thank you so much. You just gave me six months of therapy in twenty minutes. I'm so relieved."

"You're so welcome, Annie," I said. "That's the magic you hold in your fingertips. You just unblocked your 2nd Chakra and unleashed a massive flow of energy." Proceeding, I said, "I'm honored to help you relieve your pain. And I'm thrilled you uncovered a hidden wound from your past. It held all the pain of anger, disappointment, betrayal, and abandonment."

Annie's story is an excellent example of tapping on one issue, physical pain, and releasing another, emotional pain. Once she unblocked the energy, the underlying emotion had space to come through. The unconscious feeling that emerges is often the true essence of an immediate problem.

As we explore these seven energy centers, continue to notice how they occupy specific areas in your body, which I list in Chapter Two. Tune into your body as Annie did. Practice observing body sensations. Identify where the discomfort, unease, tension, or pain sits in your body. These places in your body align with your chakras. They help you pinpoint which suppressed emotions you may need to address with tapping.

Shadow Power – From Guilt to Passion, Creativity, and Joy

How do we access those Sacral Chakra gifts hidden in the negative shadows? First, we must be open to feeling our emotions instead of pushing them down. Once we address them, the blocks created by them dissipate. Then, with the path cleared, the shadows reveal their powerful gifts.

We must also embrace the *and*. In the polarities of the 2nd Chakra, it's not a case of this or that. Accepting all of ourselves, it's this *and* that. We can be so-called selfish, asking for what we want. *And* we can be generous and caring. Changing how we speak to ourselves, we say, "Sometimes I put myself first, as if I'm being selfish. But I'm not a selfish person." You reclaim your desires and release your guilt for having them.

Our 2nd Chakra shadows protect us from perceived harm by urging us to fight, flee, or freeze to survive. The shadows fight for our right to be accepted and loved for who we are, our true authentic selves. And most of us have a primary shadow that runs the show, the one we fight the hardest to contain, which accounts for how we act as adults. Following the shadow's rules, we still hide our dark sides, the behavior, ideas, and language we think are unacceptable. And we don't feel safe to let them out because we could be punished or worse.

Recognizing all the shadows hanging out in the 2nd Chakra is essential. They possess the answers to the questions we're most afraid to ask. When we clear our 2nd Chakra of blocked energy, we show up, speak, and act in a new way. We discover what we truly desire in our lives purely for us and stop feeling bad for wanting those things. A dynamic range of compelling, magnetic qualities develops from a passion for singing to writing poetry or being outdoors. Allowing our inner child to play, we can be silly and laugh at ourselves. And we can have a full-on sensual experience creating a world filled with joy, enthusiasm, and wonder.

What do you think you might uncover in your 2nd Chakra? Each of us has an authentic self, that girl we put aside long ago, who's waiting to be free. She may be four or twenty-four, and she's always been there waiting for you to attend to her needs.

Remember, shadows are the parts of us that get frightened when they sense danger. They try to get our attention by creating body sensations. Body awareness helps us handle our shadow's negative feelings faster. For instance, we might feel a little out of sorts. This symptom in the body is faint, and we tend to ignore it. However, by the next day, the feeling intensifies. We may grow impatient at minor things or get weepy. When we tune into these body signals, we recognize a need for self-care: our inner child seeks attention. If we brush her aside, she makes things worse. Physical and emotional pain can occur. In the final chapter, I share a story about one of the times my inner little one had a tantrum.

Our shadows can guide us in the healing process. And our fiercest shadow can be anger. I focused on this one shadow emotion of anger in the 2nd Chakra to emphasize its power. As mature women, we often believe we can't or shouldn't get angry. And we feel guilty if we do. Many of us vowed never to show anger because of how our angry parents frightened us. Or we have hurt others with our anger. Either way, then we're angry and feel guilty for expressing that anger. However, tapping lets us safely express this emotion. And the angry shadow doesn't go away. Instead, it transforms into passion, creativity, and joy. This energy can then flow to our 3rd Chakra.

> So, take a new approach as to how you feel emotions.
> It's not about the right emotion, or the wrong emotion.
> it's about honoring the way that you're feeling.
> We tend to think that being sensitive is a weakness,
> but it really gives us an ability to be compassionate,
> and to appreciate so many things in the world.
> —Jessica Ortner, *The Tapping Solution for
> Weight-Loss and Body Confidence*

Notes from the Basement

I AM your 2nd Chakra, the keeper of stories and feelings. Stashed here in your virtual basement, I'm a "presumed lost" storage bin. I hold a large collection of your deepest needs and biggest wishes shoved in a dark corner. Your Sacral Chakra shadows grow stronger the more you deny their existence. Trying to keep a shadow quiet only makes it louder.

Upon opening the box, you realize your childhood desires are the same things you yearn for today. Acknowledge your inner child shadow. Accept her wants and needs. Let her help you release your fear of being vulnerable. Ask for what you want and allow others to give it to you.

Put the good girl part of you aside for a while and unleash your inner wild child. Tap, rant, and throw a tantrum. Harness the released energy. Propel yourself toward your goals and dreams. Once you acknowledge your shadows, the giant energy blocks they created crumble.

Denying your dark sides, the shadows, causes blockages in your energy system.

You might be unaware of how much anger and resentment are stuffed deep inside you. However, you can follow my lead. My tapping while ranting in the car released trapped energy. Challenge yourself to vent your anger, even if you think you're not angry. And get ready for other emotions to show themselves once the energy starts to flow.

Check out Chapter Five in *Your Playbook* for the Talking to the Shadow homeplay exercise that illustrates one of the ways to open communication with this powerful part of you, your shadow.

In the next chapter, see how three seconds of courage changed me forever as we visit the virtual Great Room, the 3rd Chakra.

2nd Chakra, Notes from the Basement
https://youtu.be/VrzDZWbIExg

SCAN ME

Chapter Six

The Great Room

The 3rd Chakra – Sudden Courage

December 2012, Rincon, Georgia

"No. You don't get to talk to me that way."

Oh God, what did I do?

After his stinging verbal attack, my husband, Dennis, stood over me. His face was still red with rage. I braced myself for the worst.

Seemingly baffled by my outburst, he stopped cold and didn't say a word. You could hear a pin drop as he stepped over to his end of the couch. Then, in a single motion, he grabbed the TV remote and plopped down.

What the hell just happened?

I felt a slight sense of relief. The spinning, fearful thoughts in my head slowed down. I seldom stood up to Dennis in this way. Most of the time, I'd walk away. Dennis detested my evasion tactics, and he loved confrontation. Several people told him he should've been a lawyer. It was pointless for me even to try debating or arguing with him. At times I'd react, matching his anger. However, joining the fight only added fuel to the fire. And we'd get locked in battle.

Those three seconds of spontaneous courage were exhilarating and enlightening. They showed me a glimpse of an invisible power that was all mine. It was the power of saying "No." And I could finally say "Yes," to myself.

The Great Room

At the center of our virtual home, we find the Great Room with a vaulted ceiling above the open floor plan and large windows filling our 3rd Chakra with natural light. Here we've combined the roles of several rooms such as the living room, dining room, and office or study, into one space. There's room for every activity and at the hub, opposite those big windows, is the kitchen we revisit for the 4th Chakra.

Welcome to the Solar Plexus Chakra, located at the core of our bodies. This Chakra manages our actions and movements toward accomplishment, where we must take a deep look whenever we feel stuck.

Clutter – Blocked 3rd Chakra
Disempowering, negative impact:
low self-esteem, self-doubt, perfectionism, procrastination

"I'm sorry," I'd say as my habitual response to my husband, Dennis, and his accusations. Tiptoeing around every issue, walking on eggshells, I always tried to avoid another screaming session. Dennis was angry at the whole world, overtaken by anxiety and depression.

If I shower him with more love, I may help him get well.

I later learned that many of us often use a phrase similar to my belief. "Things will get better if I keep doing, giving, and loving more."

Meanwhile, I found myself in a codependent relationship, entangled with Dennis and all his needs. No matter what I tried, Dennis was a sinking ship. I felt the pull of him dragging me down with him. Standing up and acting on my own behalf seemed impossible to me.

At least, it seemed impossible that I would stand up to him—until I did. In that moment of boundary-setting bravery with Dennis, I spoke up for the first time. I felt my energy rise when I broke through a massive block in my 3rd Chakra. I dunked my pinky toe into the reservoir of power waiting inside me. It was an inner power I never knew existed.

The story didn't end there, though. I didn't just magically always stand up for myself from then on. As with many of us, I still had more blocks in my solar plexus to clear so I could easily access that inner power.

Our 3rd Chakra is as bright as ten thousand suns empowering us to live our best lives, healthy, prosperous, and joyful. Yet when the Solar Plexus is blocked, it shuts down, leaving us stuck. This *stuckness* happens when the rising fuel of the 2nd Chakra hits a block of massive resistance in the 3rd. This resistance is often an immediate, triggered response the moment our inner self senses an outer change. The trigger can occur even when the change is for the better, like a job offer or an invitation to go on an adventurous vacation.

Fortunately, this resistance is predictable. Every time we step toward something transformative, our inner critic fills our heads with self-doubt.

Nope, this is outside of your comfort zone. It's too risky.

Then we're prey to some of the other shadows of the 3ʳᵈ Chakra, such as procrastination, apathy, and self-sabotage. And we won't even understand why those shadows are popping up.

Sometimes, when we make progress, the blocks make us avoid appearing boastful. Still striving to prove our value, our internal monitor makes us self-conscious and hyper-vigilant about our behavior. Our minds spin with worry as tightly wound balls of negative emotion form in our stomachs. Sinking feelings of guilt, fear, and anxiety trap us in a loop of inertia. The cycle continues, and the initial self-sabotage and procrastination become habitual patterns. In time, our bodies reveal the physical effects of our deep unconscious blocks. The 3ʳᵈ Chakra problems arise in our core, from just below the ribcage to the navel. As a result, we might experience various symptoms, such as butterflies in our stomachs, nausea, gallstones, or liver disease. Fortunately, my clients quickly alleviate pain and improve their health by uncovering and clearing their hidden emotional blocks.

For example, we may decide to lose some weight for our health and appearance. We start making positive lifestyle changes to achieve our optimum weight. When we substitute carrot sticks for potato chips we think, "Wait, this doesn't feel like enough. I'm going to get hungry." And then, when we drop a few pounds and people start noticing, we often stop the healthy habits we formed. Our transformation is noticeable. And it doesn't feel safe to be visible. Therefore, progress is minimal because we backslide into old behaviors. Our body doesn't want to lose anything. The 3ʳᵈ Chakra shadow fights to keep the extra weight's protective padding. More pounds than we lost come right back on. Defeated and dejected to try another day, we repeat the gain-lose-gain-back cycle.

This same cycle can happen with trying to save money or pay off debt or other significant life changes like improving relationships, all of which can be challenging to maintain.

In addition to feelings and emotions that come up while clearing blocks in the 3rd Chakra, we return to examine our 1st and 2nd Chakras. When the energy in those first two chakras backs up, only a trickle gets through to the 3rd Chakra. Then, we're stuck in energetic quicksand, unable to step up or move forward.

Letting Go – Unblocked 3rd Chakra
Empowering, positive effect: confidence, charisma, exuberance

When our Solar Plexus obstructions clear, the rising on-fire energy of the 2nd Chakra flows up with ease. This massive energy empowers our courage to be seen as ourselves. Now we possess an enthusiastic, positive outlook for everything we do. We know why we've been stuck for so long. Inertia wanes, and we're not averse to risk-taking. As we tackle challenges, we continue to develop our sense of power. Clarity comes with ease as we continue to journey inward. It becomes easier to identify destructive or unhealthy patterns in our lives.

Through tapping, we let the inner good girl have her say. She gets to vehemently spew anger and outrage at anyone who's wronged her. And no one gets hurt. Instead, uninhibited curiosity drives us to examine our negative emotions, and kindness quiets our inner critic. This more significant charge of energy flowing through the 3rd Chakra allows us to take focused action on what matters to us.

With an unblocked Solar Plexus Chakra, we stand in our power and set healthy, personal boundaries that honor ourselves and others with ease. The world and the people around us have changed because we have transformed and strengthened our core.

Linda – 911 Call

I was in the kitchen chopping vegetables, and my phone vibrated on the counter. My client, Linda, popped onto the screen. I put down the knife to read her text, "Do you have time for a 911?"

"Yes, of course! Call now," I responded. She was another private coaching client using her 20-minute anytime coaching call between sessions. My phone immediately rang.

Linda screamed, "Oh my God, Sandy. I can't believe it."

I had to hold the phone away from my ear. "What? What's going on?"

Catching her breath, Linda said, "I just went through the drive-through ATM at my bank. You know how you had me set a goal for my account?" Not even waiting for an answer, she screamed again, "I went over it! I'm so amazed!"

"Linda, you're the amazing one," I said. "The outer success with your bank account reflects your inner work and growth. Great work with the goals we set to increase your income and savings. Remember how you felt when I suggested it was time to raise your prices?"

As she recalled that session, Linda laughed. "Yeah, writing those numbers down triggered my anxiety."

In the previous session, she said her hair salon guests were happy to pay the higher prices. And they gave her even bigger tips. A month later, she'd blown past her goal.

"Are you still hearing your father's voice?" I asked.

Linda had recently uncovered a memory of her father saying, "people like us," meaning "we can't ever earn much money." Somehow, that phrase had stuck with her, and she had unconsciously believed it all her life—until now.

"It's so funny. When I raised my rates, I did hear my father's words in my head. However, a newly empowered voice entered the conversation. It was mine, courageously responding to my father. 'Thanks, Dad. I love you. I must disagree, though, because I'm worth it.'"

Linda and I had more work to do because she had come to me to help her business prosper, *and* she wanted to be fit, slimmer, and healthier. Therefore, I guided her in an active imagination exercise during her next session. I asked her to picture herself as a child with her family at dinner time.

"How old are you in the picture? And what's going on with everyone around the table?"

"I'm eight. My father is at the head of the table to my right, eating in silence. And my mother's glaring at me from the opposite end. She was a stern disciplinarian. Like everything else, dinner had its own set of strictly enforced rules. No talking. Sit up straight. Eat what's in front of you. I was a fidgety kid, and sitting still was hard. I'm nervous just looking at this scene," she said.

I leaned toward the webcam. "I'm curious, what happens if you put your elbows on the table?"

Linda gasped, "Oh my God, my mother hit me."

"What?" I exclaimed.

"She stabbed my elbow with the serving fork," Linda said, with a surprised laugh, and a hint of anxiety.

Her mom's fork-poke hadn't harmed Linda physically. Nevertheless, the punishment taught her a message about what was acceptable at the dinner table. She had an unconscious vow to behave and consume everything on her plate. Such events can create a survival pattern in childhood that often persists into adulthood. Her present-day behavior was the result of childhood fears.

Linda stayed on her chakra awareness journey, and her protective emotional and physical walls came down in time. Working with her shadows, Linda released the pounds as she wished. Additionally, her income and profits grew beyond her expectations by using my specialized wealth tapping. I'm impressed by Linda and her accomplishments. She's living a happy, healthy, prosperous, and dream-filled life.

Shadow Power – From Inaction to Action and Healthy Boundaries

Stepping up and making progress in self-improvement awakens fears in our 3rd Chakra shadows. Afraid of change, our shadows get triggered into procrastination or self-sabotage. "It's not safe to put yourself out there," they whisper. As a result, we can succumb to inertia and inactivity.

Whatever fears you have, they are signs. For instance, if public speaking frightens you, that's because your inner child is cowering in the shadow of your Solar Plexus. She holds the memories of what happened to you when you were about eight. Perhaps you were one of those kids whose face flushed red when you stood at the front of the third-grade class. Maybe you had to read out loud. You thought you'd upchuck your lunch on your desk as you stumbled over the words. Or your hand shook as you tried to solve a math problem on the blackboard and you dropped the chalk. Still today, your stomach churns the second you know that you must speak publicly. If you've been afraid to use your voice for most of your life, as I was, you may not speak up for yourself at all.

Fear can show up as our most significant block—procrastination—a typical 3rd Chakra shadow, the direct opposite of action. We yearn to achieve worthwhile goals, yet we often drag our feet with distractions. Born of perfectionism, at procrastination's core is fear. Fear of failure, criticism, or ridicule simmers just below conscious awareness. From there, the inner critic and self-doubt step in. We beat ourselves up for lack of accomplishment, blame poor time management skills, and think we're lazy.

When we dig deep enough, we uncover the true nature of our procrastination. This shadow is our rebel with its hands on its hips saying, "Don't tell me what to do."

Wow, no wonder I struggle with motivation. My inner rebel is in charge.

We can free each shadow from the fear it holds—simply by befriending it. I know, you might think, *this is too much woo woo.* Hear me out! It's possible to converse with our shadows. Meeting my shadows helped me get out of a rut. Whether it feels crazy or not, acknowledging our shadows unblocks energy. That boost bolsters our courage. When we stand in our authentic power, we can take action.

I learned the process of talking to our shadows from Epic Life Coach Fiona Orr. During a group coaching session, she gave us a writing exercise to list our negative emotions and beliefs.

Good Lord, my list is long. I'm a mess.

Fiona instructed us to give our emotions names to help us visualize speaking to them. I closed my eyes and saw my shadows, remembering a scene from the original *Westside Story* movie. Snapping their fingers, a street gang strode in unison toward me. Then the image morphed into the Bruno Mars music video, "Uptown Funk." There she was, my Procrastination Woman, aka Rebel Rita, leading the pack. I learned to befriend her. And now, when I feel myself resisting even things I want to do, I ask Rebel Rita what's going on. Once she can express the fears and self-doubt, I help her cooperate with me to make progress. At last, when Rebel Rita and I are in harmony, I step into action and approach life with enthusiasm.

Talking to your shadows may still sound ludicrous to you. Nevertheless, it's imperative to understand how our shadows' voices create behavior patterns and toxic habits. Those voices in our minds prevent us from taking steps out of our very uncomfortable comfort zone. Our shadows are strong. When we ignore an emotion or feeling, the shadow tries harder to get our attention. If we don't respond to overwhelm, the shadow gives us frustration. When we still ignore the emotion, our shadows don't give up. If overwhelm and frustration aren't working, they send in anxiety and fear, fear, fear to stop us from what they see as life-threatening risks.

In what ways do you stop yourself from becoming your authentic self? Most of my clients come to me overwhelmed and exhausted. Yet even though they're fatigued, they're not sleeping through the night. These symptoms are blocked 3rd Chakra signals. How do you feel? Stop and listen to your answer. What's not okay or could be better? That's your clue to look more closely to find a shadow.

Don't just look for things that are not great habits, like procrastination. Many of us show our love by doing for others and giving our time and energy. And we feel good about it. However, over-giving can catch up with us and awaken our shadows. "Something's gotta give," and it's most often our health. We only give ourselves permission to say "No" when we are sick or injured. Telling my husband that he couldn't speak to me in such a cruel way was the first time I put my foot down. I finally stood up for myself.

The 3rd Chakra regulates how we step into action, including standing strong and setting boundaries. In the safety of a tapping session, we're clearing the blocks in our Solar Plexus Chakra that keep us inactive by tapping, ranting, and letting it all out with vehemence.

Miracles happen when we practice tapping and ranting. This over-the-top technique moves the stuck energy and clears the air. I know it can sound far-fetched. However, it works. When we're upset with someone, we change the other person's energy by tapping, even without direct contact. The next time we see or speak to them, they've changed; the dynamic is different, with less friction.

For instance, a woman yearned to hear from her son after three long years of estrangement. In our sessions, she couldn't express rage against him; she felt only sadness. Then, hesitant at first, she tapped and ranted about her disappointment in her son. Something shifted. Two days later, out of the blue, her son called her. He was different. No longer feeling malice toward his mother, he wanted to come home for a visit. The miracle of moving negative energy brought mother and son together. They both let go of past wounds.

> If you are to thrive, you must participate
> in the evolution of your body's energy patterns.
> —Donna Eden, *Energy Medicine*

Notes from the Great Room

As your 3rd Chakra, I keep you stuck when the energy flow is blocked. When this happens, you must examine your belief system. Do you operate under a misbelief that you must think and behave in specific ways? Do you hold yourself back, afraid to shine your light? Are you attending to everyone else's whims while disregarding your own? It's time to give yourself tough love—self-love and self-respect fuel empowerment.

The energy blocks in the Solar Plexus clear when you learn to set healthy personal boundaries. There's a reason you need to put your oxygen mask on first. It's a matter of survival. The rising blaze of 2ⁿᵈ Chakra energy flowing into an open 3ʳᵈ Chakra strengthens your courage.

Standing up for yourself, you declare your value and release the guilt of taking care of yourself. By letting go of the vows to be invisible, you honor yourself as special and unique. You hold a new understanding: You can have flaws and also be awesome. Celebrating your right to shine allows everyone else to do the same. Your decision to purchase this book is a 3ʳᵈ Chakra action. Making this choice, you took a step toward taking control of your life. The voice in your head says, "I'm going for it."

Ready to stop getting in your own way? I've got you covered in *Your Woo Woo Way Playbook* with a new variation of the tapping we've done together so far. With the Stepping into Action process, you get to the root of what's holding you back and transform it into a supportive force.

In the next chapter, discover how much we need our new-found courage when the energy flows up to the 4ᵗʰ Chakra, The Heart.

3ʳᵈ Chakra, Notes from the Great Room
https://youtu.be/DPynpcA1vn4

The Kitchen

The 4ᵗʰ Chakra – The Forgiving Heart

June 2017, Natick, Massachusetts
Intuitive Chakra Mastery Certification Workshop, Day 4
with Margaret Lynch Raniere

"We're staying until we both have a breakthrough," Kathleen said. She crossed her arms and gave me a mischievous grin. "Are you in?"

Meeting her gaze, I said, "Game on, partner. Let's do this."

Kathleen and I remained in our seats as the event attendees shuffled out of the hotel ballroom. It felt as if we were staying after school. There was an air in the room of exhaustion and exhilaration from the deep transformational work we'd done. However, she and I weren't finished. We had been partners for the tapping exercises, and we both struggled with blocked Heart Chakras. We wanted to make every effort to release our internal blocks.

Kathleen asked me to first guide her through the Heart Chakra clearing process, which was a series of tapping and visualizations. She blamed herself for the distress occurring in her second marriage. And she believed she would never have the loving relationship she craved. Kathleen tapped along with me, letting herself feel deep sadness and loss.

Within a few minutes, Kathleen's energy shifted. Then, exhaling a long, deep breath, she sighed. "I get it now. Misconceptions cloud my mind, even though I know I'm doing the best I can."

"Of course, you are. You broke through your wall of resistance, and your heart opened," I said. "Now, bring in some compassion. You've suffered enough. And you deserve better."

Kathleen wiped her tears and gave me a confident smile. She said, "For the first time in a long while, I have hope. And it's not only for my marriage. It's for me."

We hugged, and then it was my turn to be on the receiving end. I also had angst over issues with my husband.

Please, subconscious mind, show me what I need to see.

Kathleen first asked me a question about a past mistake. "What's your biggest unforgivable mistake? The big one that you never forgave yourself for? And do you believe you don't deserve forgiveness?"

It was easy to picture the mistake because it was always in the back of my mind. And it would pop into the forefront at any given moment. Kathleen and I tapped as I talked to the younger version of myself. "I hate you," I said. "You're so weak. You're so naïve and stupid. It's unacceptable. I can't forgive you." Then, starting to cry and continuing to tap, I said, "You made a huge mistake. And you kept repeating it. It's unforgivable."

Kathleen guided me through all the self-judgment and the heavy, unrelenting guilt I carried inside me. I gasped for breath as the silent tears became outright sobs. My heart burned in my throat. The tapping kept me grounded in my body and silenced my fear of being too emotional. Instead, my tears and sobs released a massive charge of trapped energy.

Finally, I could heal.

Kathleen said, "Go back to the picture where you're still making the big mistake. How does it look to you now? What's different?"

My invisible yet impenetrable armor was still up. Crying through the tapping, I said, "I can't let this go." "It's too bad." "Why didn't I do something different?" "The price was too high." "It cost me so much." "It's unforgivable." "I don't know how to get out of this."

I tapped through a stockpile of emotional blocks as Kathleen instructed me. "With your inner vision, step back and observe the situation," she said. "What was going on around you back then? Who else was involved? Were there any external influences?"

Taking a bold look back gave me a new perspective. I saw the price I'd paid and what blaming myself for years had done. A smidgen of compassion slipped through the crack in my heart.

"Now imagine entering the picture as your adult self today," said Kathleen. "Put your arm around mistake-making younger Sandy, and keep tapping."

That day, Kathleen and I tapped through waves of agonizing sadness, regret, grief, and loss as I envisioned my younger self with me.

Oh God, I'm still crying.

I could never get that time back. My grief was over the loss of what might have been. I finally gave myself a break and honored everything I had gone through. And an epiphany surfaced from underneath the regret. I understood that I did the best that I could at the time. I would not waste another minute suffering from guilt.

The flood of tears stopped. Feeling the energy rise within my core, I sat up taller. The tapping process brought me to self-forgiveness and self-love. Kathleen and I ended the session with the final phrase, "I deserve better."

A feeling of lightness came over me as I released the emotional weight of grief. The image of my husband, Dennis, faded off the screen in my mind's eye. At least for that moment, I let him go.

The burden of long-held negative beliefs had lifted for Kathleen and me. I wish we had before and after photos of us. Our circumstances hadn't changed, yet we were different. With inner strength, we walked with confidence as we left the ballroom.

Reclaiming My Heart

My shifts from the Chakra Mastery Workshop rejuvenated my body, mind, and spirit. With a renewed trust in the power of tapping, I committed to using it often. It's been over five years since that experience, and I recognize tapping's continuing tremendous impact on my life.

At the time, however, I didn't know I had such an impenetrable wall around my heart. My 1st Chakra shadow was vigilant. It wanted to protect me from ever getting hurt again. As a result, this foundational block obstructed the rest of the other chakras above, and the power went out in my virtual *Inner House of Me*. I was running on empty.

During my previous months of tapping training, I had made gradual progress in removing blocks in my system. However, the workshop intensive and the practice session with Kathleen created my most significant breakthrough. Brick by brick, chakra by chakra, the wall crumbled. A month after the event, I opened my heart to someone new, unafraid to give and receive love again. With an unblocked Heart Chakra, the free-flowing energy in me affected everything. The grief moved. I stopped blaming myself.

My husband, Dennis, passed away in peace. In my heart, I know he felt my positive, energetic shift. Both of us could let go. And I anticipated an adventurous, abundant future.

The Kitchen

Food isn't the only thing prepared, served, and consumed in our virtual kitchen. Your 4th Chakra, the Heart Chakra, invites you to pull up a chair and join it at the kitchen table. We nourish ourselves and each other in this supportive, loving space. Often called the home's heartbeat, this chakra nurtures and sustains us, strengthening our bodies, minds, and spirits. Coffee and late-night refrigerator raids mingle with computer time and creative projects.

Our kitchens often buzz with activity. Our senses awaken with the rich aroma of fresh-brewed coffee wafting through the room. Stovetop sizzles compete for attention with clinking dishware, keyboard clicks, and music from cellphone videos. And yet sometimes, our best moments occur when we're alone in this space with our thoughts.

The Heart Chakra embodies the kitchen energetic dimension, filled with love and appreciation and may also hold the sadness of loss and disappointment. Taking time to go within and be with this part of ourselves is crucial. Otherwise, our hearts may break—in every sense of the word.

Our upper and lower chakra energy merges in the 4th Chakra, similar to how the kitchen pulls our days together. With an open heart, empowerment energy enters from below. And flowing from above is manifestation energy. Positioned between the upper and lower chakras, The Heart Chakra is an engine pumping energy from above and below—it's the heart of our energy system.

Inoperable Kitchen – Blocked 4th Chakra
Disempowering, negative impact:
grief, self-criticism, co-dependence, jealousy, fear of betrayal

Because the Heart Chakra is located where the lower and upper chakras intersect, with a blocked 4th Chakra, we receive a two-way traffic jam. Remember, if the engine is clogged, the flow of energy is impeded in both directions, leaving the 4th Chakra underdeveloped.

When we avoid essential work in the lower chakras, the 4th Chakra shifts into negativity. Imagine it as a kitchen hearth without firewood or other fuel; our cold hearts shut down. Then, the blocked Heart Chakra hardens us. With no warmth, we grow cold and cynical. Defending the condition of our hearts, we armor up with criticism and judgment of ourselves and others. Behind a wall of self-protection, we hide behind our dense, solid boundaries. *Nothing, and no one gets in.* We reject offers of help from people who care about us. Trying to protect ourselves from more heartbreak, we turn away from the love we crave.

Then, the unconscious memories of past wounds and disappointments awaken our shadows. As soon as the shadows sense a threat, they fortify the wall and strengthen our resistance. Our hearts harden with scars from repeated let-downs, broken promises, and lost opportunities. Unconscious resistance—on auto-pilot—pushes back creative energy from the Solar Plexus when it tries to light the fire.

Excessive highly-charged energy can also block the 4th Chakra, enlarging our Heart Chakra. Receiving this outsized energy can feel warm and supportive. However, it often develops into self-centeredness, meddling, or codependency. We might try to compensate for the love we never received as children. Or our boundaries with others become porous. Instead of an impenetrable wall, we may have one that permits anything and anyone to get through, turning us into doormats.

In either case, the wall serves its purpose without discrimination—repelling our ability to speak our truth, imagine infinite possibilities, and connect with the Conscious Universe. Therefore, neither our upper nor lower chakras' energy can get through to our hearts.

There's no chance of breaking through those emotional wounds except to experience the whole level of compassion and love that our hearts can hold—to be open to forgiveness in all forms.

The Heart of Forgiveness – Unblocked 4th Chakra
Empowering, positive effect: love, compassion, empathy, connectedness

The average home's kitchen has a four-burner stove for cooking. Likewise, our Heart Chakra manages four levels of healing forgiveness. Working through them is vital to our happiness. Approach each forgiveness level with care. Adapt nonjudgmental curiosity as you examine what your heart holds within it.

The first level often comes easy—brushing minor transgressions aside. In general, it's the right thing to do when we let things go. In the grand scheme, an offense isn't worth fretting over. "No problem," we say. "It's okay. No worries."

At the second level of forgiveness, we need our day in virtual court; before pointing the finger at others, it's important to tap and rant first. While tapping and ranting, we shout, voicing our pain, hurling blame at the people and circumstances that wounded our hearts. Then, we start fleshing things out a little more. That's how we break through the wall around our heavily-guarded hearts. In this way, a deeper level of healing takes place.

Reaching the third level of forgiveness is difficult due to our unconscious resistance because we must pardon *ourselves*. Each of us can recall mistakes we've made in our lives. However, self-forgiveness often eludes us in favor of self-blame. Disguised as truth, words from our inner critics overpower us. We parrot and personalize their comments, saying, "It was all my fault; I should've known better; I could've done better. I was naïve and stupid." Then we pack away our regret and stuff it down. As a result, our seemingly unforgivable mistakes can lie dormant, festering for years.

Many of us are tormented by guilt, even for things that happened in childhood. When I tell my clients to imagine being back at the scene of their "crime," I'm no longer surprised by how young they were—usually six or seven. And yes, sometimes we carry errors from later in our lives—our teens, twenties, thirties, and beyond. Our self-blame sounds reasonable no matter what age we were when these things happened. We continue to point our fingers inward, thinking social order would agree.

Our inner judge and jury unconsciously sentence us to a lifetime of self-inflicted punishment. Then, we wonder why there's so much negativity and suffering in our lives. Our primary thoughts are, *I must deserve it. It's the story of my life, and I can't change it.* Holding onto the heavy burden of our obvious screwup, we presume there's no way out. And yet, there is a way—the path of self-forgiveness. As the spiritual teacher and best-selling author Kyle Gray says, "We must face our own darkness." Doing so is the key to unblocking our Heart Chakra.

Everyone isn't always excited about this third level of forgiveness. I often hear clients say, "I'm fine. What happened made me who I am today." That's not the same as forgiveness. So, the next time you start blaming yourself, stop. Instead, take a moment to feel your heart. You might sense a physiological rumble beneath your stoic exterior. We can't say, "I'm okay," with conviction, unless we acknowledge the darkest parts of ourselves. Otherwise, a volcano of sadness or anger and rage can erupt at any moment.

Two interesting characters in the fourth level of forgiveness can facilitate those eruptions: the inner bully and the inner child. For the most part, we'd prefer not to interact with either of these temperaments because they mirror unacknowledged parts of ourselves. They are necessary for the fourth level's task of self-acceptance and self-forgiveness. For example, instead of stuffing down your inner child's neediness, notice how you would feel saying, "I have a needy side. But I'm not a needy person." Or, instead of rejecting the inner bully's strength, we say, "I've got strength. But I'm not a bully." As we accept the many layers of ourselves, we become compassionate and well-rounded, both strong *and* soft. I share more about these two characters in discussing your 4th Chakra's shadow power.

Once we forgive ourselves and others, the walls around our hearts crumble and fall. The heart opens when we break through its blocks. Our senses heighten, and we fall in love with life. Other people feel our energy and notice us more. Feeling more aliveness, our world becomes warm and friendly. And our open hearts mean we're available for the love we've craved for so long—now love can reach us, and we can receive love.

Open lower chakras allow empowerment energy to flow unencumbered into the Heart Chakra. An unblocked Root Chakra helps us feel safe to give and receive love. Our wants, needs, and burning desires ignite in an open 2nd Chakra to fuel our passion and creativity. And strength, determination, and courage of the 3rd Chakra flow unrestricted. This free-flowing energy blasts through to an open heart. Once we learn to clear the lower chakras, wisdom, compassion, understanding, and patience flow from the upper chakras to fill our Heart Chakras.

Shadow Power – From Grief to Love and Self-Compassion

Our shadows can maneuver through the clogged energy channels to the heart. With shape-shifting prowess, they show up unannounced, carrying all their baggage with them. They weigh on our hearts as forms of grief, the daemon of the Heart Chakra. As a result, our virtual kitchen fills with smoky sadness. Discouragement and unworthiness lurk in this fog of disappointment.

Our shadows often awaken with the passing of someone we love. The weight of sadness and loss can leave us depressed and heartbroken. Physiologically, grief creates a chemical reaction in the heart muscle that causes intense physical pain. It's an experience of double-edged mourning. When grief hits hard, it feels like a knife has stabbed our hearts. Yet, our wounded souls hurt even more.

There's no specific definition or timetable for grief. No matter how many stages they tell us there should be, the grief process can be messy. Gray emotions wash over us like ocean waves. They softly lap as we move along with the little ripples. And then, without warning, an internal storm churns up our feelings. The waves hit again, crashing down with a fierce intensity. This cycle repeats an unknown number of times with each loss. Therefore, we must take as much time as we need to restabilize through grief. While grief doesn't go away, with time, it does soften. Then, when we can arrive at self-forgiveness and self-compassion, we form the glue to mend our shattered hearts. And the key is to tap when the waves roll in.

The work with our grief shadow extends to unacknowledged lower chakra shadows. Born out of childhood fears and losses, this part of us constricts the heart wall. The shadows add more protective blocks to the barricade whenever we're hurt, walling us in. We make giving to others a specialty, which depletes our energy further. Afraid to open up and maybe get hurt again, our hearts close. We suffer inside a self-constructed prison of grief.

If we lose a job, a home, or another opportunity, we suffer grief and its spinoffs of sadness, denial, and anger. The cost is high. A blocked Heart Chakra freezes us in and others out. Lost and isolated, we're stuck and believe we're unworthy of love.

The best way to escape our inner jail is to understand the impact of blockages below the Heart Chakra. Therefore, we must go back to the lower levels. You can revisit Chapters Four, Five, and Six of *The Woo Woo Way* and *Your Playbook*. Learn from the lower chakra shadows how to accept and love them. Does it sound implausible? After all, even thinking about our shadows, we feel self-judgment and condemnation.

Well, the trick is that these parts of us interpret threats when they sense what feels "unacceptable." And when we instead practice acceptance, the shadows dissipate. We relieved them of their jobs as jailers.

Ready to give shadow acceptance a try? Let's think of one for you. Recall a person who gets on your nerves in a big way. Their behavior infuriates you. It's despicable. And you wonder how anybody could consistently conduct themselves in that way.

Who pops into your mind's eye? I bet they have one of two distinct shadow characteristics.

The first shadow is an insecure weakling who acts helpless with an irritating high-pitched whiney voice. They're annoying as hell. You bite your lip to refrain from shouting, "Get a grip already!" Guess what's going on? This personality type triggers your inner child's neediness shadow. Most of us strive to keep this part of us at bay. Showing vulnerability and need is not a good look, and we refuse to succumb to it. The only way we allow others to see us as having any need is when we're sick. And I mean down and out, sick-in-bed, sick. When we're tired, stressed, or in pain, we tell everyone, "I've got this."

No matter what, weakness is not an option. Yet we all have this side of ourselves.

The emotional pushback on neediness takes a tremendous amount of energy. Our body weakens under strain, often taking us down with an actual illness. Whether it's a case of the flu, an injury, or a catastrophic disease, that's the only time we can stop. It's the one time we say "No."

The second shadow is a mean, obnoxious, loudmouth bully that takes over the space in our heads. The thought of this type of character makes our stomachs churn. *There's no way I could ever be as arrogant and narcissistic.* This personality lauds over others with intimidation and fear tactics. Flaunting privilege and abusing power, they stomp on anyone who gets in their way. We're baffled by anybody who admires them—even though part of us is a little like them. That part of us would like to stand up and tell someone how we feel. To take a stand and be assertive. Then, we often reject those impulses because we don't want anyone to accuse us of being the bully.

Whether too weak or too overbearing, we find these undesirable traits despicable. This judgment of others (and that part of ourselves) affects our relationships with friends, families, and associates. Rejecting those shadows, we cannot see the gifts they bring.

What, they have gifts?

To see their gifts, let's observe these characters again. Notice how they reflect the inner child and inner bully from the fourth level of forgiveness? How might their behavior patterns benefit them? Consider either persona. There's a bit of cunning in how they operate. Weak people expend little energy when they want something. They only need to ask others for help. Couldn't we use some of that willingness to ask for help sometimes? If a needy person bugs you, ask yourself, "What are the wants and needs I've denied in my life?" Notice how this person's childlike voice reflects your inner child.

She's asking for what you never got. And you still don't feel worthy enough to ask for it.

You don't want to appear vulnerable. Yet those 2nd Chakra needs, such as wanting to be seen, heard, appreciated, and loved, are still within you. We have all sorts of unmet needs lodged in our hearts. I'm not asking you to turn into a messy, needy person. It's about reclaiming a lost part of ourselves and being open to receive our heart's desire.

Begin to give your inner child a voice to ask for what she wants. Proceed with one tiny request at a time. For example, see what happens when you allow yourself to ask for a hug. Your little inner child is yearning for it.

Now let's check out the overbearing bully. Once, someone told me I got upset by an aggressive person because something in me attracted her to me.

What? Are you kidding me? I felt the exact opposite. *I'm just an easy target. They intimidate the crap out of me.*

Nevertheless, instead of fighting them in my head, I had to come around to understanding the behavior I didn't like. If we harness the power of this kind of character, we stop playing small. Instead, we show up, speak up for ourselves, and act on our intentions.

Harnessing the positive benefits from both shadows is possible. And the fourth level of forgiveness work helps us claim the gifts these polarizing behaviors bring. It takes courage to look within our Heart Chakra and forgive our shadow sides. Even so, it's the fastest way to quiet our inner critic. Judgment and bitterness are left behind.

Potent shadow work soothes the soul. The forgiveness process with tapping heals our hearts. Shining a light into the dark gives voice to the shadow, that heartbroken part of us, and exposes repressed grief.

Tending to our past wounds and mistakes with salves of forgiveness removes the overbearing weight of trauma.

When a wall of resistance encloses your 4th Chakra, you may think your heart is unfixable. Instead, you protect yourself from the pain of disappointment. However, this divine aha moment comes from within your heart. It's calling you to turn on your love light. You deserve better. Breaking through blocks of unworthiness opens us to compassion and understanding. When the Heart Chakra clears, the energy moves. And there's a sudden energetic breakthrough, an epiphany. You realize when your heart broke, it broke open. The key to healing your Heart Chakra is radical forgiveness.

Melissa and the Cat

Ding. Glancing at my phone, I saw an incoming message from a new client, Melissa. Four days earlier, during her initial discovery call, she expressed overwhelm with frustration, anxiety, fear, and feeling "stuck." She opted for my six-month coaching package and scheduled with me the following week.

"Do you ever take 911 calls before a first coaching session?" she asked in her text.

Well, this is a first.

I agreed Melissa could have a 911 call and soon rang her number.

"I'm hoping you can tap with me. I'm really hurting right now. And I think I'm gonna lose it."

"Sure, Melissa, that's what this call is for, so tell me what's going on," I said.

"You might think this is crazy," said Melissa, crying. "My sweet old cat, Raven, is failing, and it's killing me."

"Oh, I'm so sorry, Melissa. That's so hard. She's your baby."

She was crying so hard she couldn't catch her breath. Through the sobs, Melissa said, "I know she's old, nineteen. She's been with me since she was a kitten. I can't bear to let her go. And I don't want her to suffer either."

My eyes filled with tears thinking of my beloved Josie. Finally, I said, "Okay, Melissa, take a breath. Feel your feet. Move your fingers. And start tapping."

Anxious thoughts and fears spilled out of her. We tapped on her sadness over the imminent loss of her treasured kitty. In a few minutes, Melissa was calmer. She regained composure. As we continued to tap, a more intense emotion emerged, which often happens. Once we address the current problem, another deeper issue pops up from underneath it.

Still sniffling, Melissa revealed that she'd lost three important people in her life. One was in childhood, and the other two were recent. "I don't know why this is coming up now," she said.

That's the kind of thing clients say when an associated memory emerges, exposing another buried feeling in a sudden recollection of an event. Their prevailing current emotions have a direct link to a past event. The shadow of grief about the impending loss of a treasured pet triggered the unexpressed sadness and loss already dwelling in Melissa's aching heart.

Once her emotions found this window to express themselves, they had more to say. I knew Melissa's Heart Chakra held the most significant blocks on her path to getting unstuck. However, she needed to unblock her lower energy centers first.

In the initial sessions, I guided Melissa through those chakras to clear away long-buried wounds. Her heart had been broken many times over failed relationships, lost time, and lost money. And now she was devastated by her dear cat's recent passing.

A dense wall blocked Melissa's Heart Chakra. Even though she yearned to find a new loving relationship, nobody was getting in. However, she was determined to do the deep work and ready to make a change. I held a container of safety for Melissa as she uncovered years of hidden programmed beliefs. Her inner child spoke of painful wounds. And although she was scared, she allowed the grief shadow in her heart to voice her unforgivable mistake. Then, with compassion, Melissa found self-forgiveness.

Through these processes of empowerment and transformation, Melissa reclaimed her authentic self. She reached out to friends and started socializing again. She enrolled in an impromptu dance class. And a chance encounter led to an incredible budding romance. Once her heart began to heal, Melissa radiated enthusiasm and joy. She manifested a wonderful life with the man of her dreams. While I can't guarantee every transformation to be this spectacular, it certainly can be.

There is no greater agony than bearing an untold story inside you.
—Maya Angelou, *I Know Why the Caged Bird Sings*

Love Letter from The Kitchen

I'm an open kitchen, and walls don't work for me. They impede the flow of my on-fire energy, passion, and creativity to the rest of the house.

An impenetrable wall around your heart can obstruct your energetic power supply. Then stagnation begins. Stuck in an uncomfortable comfort zone, you withhold love from yourself and others. If you long for peace, love, and joy, you must look at what in your life feels like a struggle. Then ask, "Can I forgive myself?" "Have I endured enough punishment?" I bet you have.

The 4th Chakra opens us to a world of love in all forms when unblocked. We accept and forgive the parts of us that made mistakes. We no longer deflect compliments, thinking we don't deserve them. Our empowerment energy channel is open from the Root Chakra to the Heart Chakra. We see the world as a kinder place because we embody the essence of love. And we continue to attract love in all its forms to us.

Now it's time to do an excellent tapping homeplay exercise that reduces stress and helps you sleep. Go to Chapter Seven of *Your Playbook* and do the Healing Your Heart homeplay exercise. Let go of old stories and fill your heart with love and appreciation.

Watch your step as we move upstairs and inspect the nooks of our virtual renovation house. Let's tour the essential upper chakras in The House of You. How clear do you feel in your upper chakras? Do you have confident self-expression? Can you trust your intuition? What level of understanding and consciousness might you reach?

Let's find out.

4th Chakra, A Love Letter from the Kitchen
https://youtu.be/8X5O8N4elZE

Chapter Eight

The Mezzanine

The 5th Chakra – From the Barn to the Belt

Summer 1957, Old Pekin Hill Road, Rural Western New York State

"What in God's name did you think you were doing?" my mother bellowed, looming over me, hands on her hips, glaring down at me.

I didn't say a word.

Later, in my teen years, I would call scenes like this one The Kitchen Inquisition, with a blinding light in the ceiling and my mother glaring, waiting for an explanation.

That morning started as usual. However, it was about to change with a drastic turn of events.

First, I did my daily chore, gathering eggs from the low-roofed chicken coop. Then, after leaving the basket on the kitchen counter and eating the bowl of oatmeal my mom put on the table, I headed for the woods to walk along the stream. I felt giddy at the possibility of catching some pollywogs and spotting unusual birds. I loved being by myself in nature's quiet space.

Grape vineyards and orchards surrounded the house we lived in, and the sweet scent of blooming fruit trees wafted through the air in the spring, foretelling the massive crop of apples, peaches, pears, plums, and cherries.

My mom instigated our family's moves, always looking for somewhere better, and my dad went along with it. That year, my siblings and I lived with our parents on a fruit farm out in the country on the short side of an L-shaped ranch house on a hill overlooking the farm.

The Fletchers and their daughter, Rebecca (Becca to me), occupied the longest part of the L. I'm unsure if being the same age, almost six, was a blessing or curse. Her adventurous spirit often led to mischief and misadventures. For instance, sometimes Becca and I grew tired of climbing trees and gorging on ripe fruit. Then she'd say, "Come on, let's go!" and march us across the road to become Lilliputians snacking in the strawberry field.

Halfway to the woods, Becca's yell suddenly interrupted my thoughts of exploring the stream.

"Hey, wait up," she called, running after me. "Let's do something different today."

Red-gold pigtails blew across her freckled face. She was an antsy kid with an active imagination and was always on the move. Something inside me told me to keep walking. Nevertheless, I couldn't ignore her. I turned toward her, wondering what she'd dreamt up for us this time.

"Oh, okay, Becca. What do you wanna do?" I asked.

She grinned, exposing the wide gap where there used to be two front teeth. "I wanna show you something. It's fun."

Following her, Becca led me into the cow barn. We weren't supposed to be there. Even though the cows were out to pasture and the barn was empty, we gagged on the stench of manure and sour milk. The stalls where they milked the cows ran lengthwise along the sides of the barn, each connected to an automated watering system. The cows accessed water by pushing their noses against a metal lever, which Rebecca had discovered, and she wanted to play.

"Wow, the cows have water fountains," I exclaimed.

Rebecca giggled. "Tee hee, watch this." Her fingers played in the water as she pushed a lever several times. Then her eyes grew big. "Let's push them all," she squealed, skipping from one to another, down one side and up the other.

I crinkled my nose and called after her, "Um, I don't know, Becca."

Looking back, Becca taunted me. "Oh, come on. It's fun. Don't be a weenie." She yelped and jumped with glee as she pushed the next lever. Then, spellbound, she watched the water pouring.

Becca's crazy! She acts like she's never seen water before.

I swallowed the fear, knowing I was about to do something wrong. Finally, I found courage, reached up, and pushed hard on the lever. Cold water streamed out, filling the small water bowl. I felt cool playing along with Becca. Even so, I didn't get why she was so excited.

"Wait, Becca, something's wrong! The water's not stopping! It won't turn off." I started panicking.

The levers were stuck. An overflow trough caught the water spilling over the edge of the bowls. We stood back for a minute and watched. The water kept flowing, and there was no containing it.

"The barn is flooding!" I cried. "How do we turn it off? What do we do?"

My nervous stomach churned.

I should run right now and find somebody to turn off the water.

Instead, I froze.

I can't tell Becca that I'm afraid. She's gonna laugh and call me a weenie. I want her to like me and prove I can be adventurous too.

Becca pivoted away from me, turning toward the barn door. Her pigtails bounced in unison off her shoulders. "It's fine. My dad can fix it when he comes in," she chirped as if it was no big deal. Then, just outside the barn door, something caught her eye. "Hey, look," Becca stopped, pointing at the oat bin, "let's hide inside here."

Once again, I followed her. We crawled inside and snuggled down in the full bin of dusty oats. The smell reminded me of oatmeal cooking on the stove, and I thought, *am I lying in my breakfast?*

Maybe they won't figure out it was us who flooded the barn.

Becca soon fell asleep, spent from her hyperkinetic morning. I was too scared to shut my eyes. Meanwhile, our families and neighbors were looking everywhere for us two lost little girls. They searched in ever-widening circles, wondering if we'd gotten hurt somehow. Or worse, what if someone took us? I could hear people getting closer and calling out for us. Becca slept undisturbed, oblivious. Meanwhile, I was wide awake and afraid to move. Fear and a painful lump in my throat stopped me from making a sound for a long time.

They saw what we've done. I know we're in big trouble.

Becca woke up, at last, rested from our escapades. Together, we pushed the bin's heavy lid open and crawled out of the oats. She patted her belly. "I'm starving. It must be time for dinner." She seemed oblivious to any consequences we might be facing.

Meanwhile, I had no appetite. We were in that bin for hours. I knew Becca's parents would laugh at her antics and call her a rascal. But, on the other hand, my mother had no sense of humor.

Skipping back to the house, I followed more reluctantly, dreading what was to come. The neighbors called out when they saw us. Then I heard my mother yelling from the back stoop, and her voice carried over the farm fields and down the road.

"Sandra Suzanne, get in this house right now!" She sounded furious

I trudged inside, head down, anticipating interrogation and fearing the worst—punishment.

I wanna get out of here, away from her. I'm terrified, with my feet frozen to the kitchen floor.

My mother was frantic when they couldn't find me. Now that she knew I was okay, she was angry. Grabbing The Belt, she glared at me. Nobody wore the big, thick, black leather belt. Instead, Mom reserved it for special punishment, teaching us a lesson. "Unacceptable behavior brings consequences," she'd preach. In my mother's world, unacceptable meant the belt.

"And for Christ's sake, open your mouth and speak. I have to put my hand on your head to see if you're nodding yes or no."

My throat burned, I couldn't speak, and my eyes welled up with tears. I wanted to run to my father for safety. But he was sitting in the living room, ignoring the situation and doing his crossword puzzle. I was confused because he usually did that after dinner. The familiar smells of cooking dinner were missing because they'd been looking for me.

Looking up at my mom, I tried to tell her I was sorry. However, my feeble attempt came out like hiccups instead of an apology. Finally, gasping between sobs, I choked out, "I'm suh-huh-har-ee." My constricted throat strangled the words into weeps. Mom looked so big and intimidating. I didn't think I could get any smaller. I did, though, and dreaded what might come next. Even though I knew my mom loved me, whenever she got angry, I got out of the way and stayed quiet. This time there was no hiding.

"I'm sorry doesn't cut it, young lady," she said, staring at me. "And quit your crying, or I'll give you something to cry about," she warned.

I'd seen her lash out at my older siblings before. However, until then, I'd never heard her intense, harsh tone directed toward me. My tears seemed to flow like water, like in the flooded barn. There was no way I could stop.

"There's no dinner because of you." Then, clutching the belt, she growled, "Go to your room. Now."

I crept upstairs and climbed into bed. I still slept in a crib even though I'd turn six next month. Mom kept the guardrails up halfway. I lay there shaking, hoping the belt in her hand was only a threat.

No such luck. I heard my mom's heavy footsteps as she stomped up the rickety wooden stairs a minute later. I could hear the dangling belt buckle clanking against the wall on her way up. Then, her tall shadow loomed in the doorway. "You need to learn your lesson, young lady. Pull down your bottoms and get on your stomach."

Obeying her command, I tightened my trembling, skinny body, bracing for the blows.

Belt in hand, my mother reached over the rails to strike my behind. "This is gonna hurt me more than you," she said sternly.

Really?

She must have held back her full strength, not wanting to injure my tiny frame because, thankfully, after only three strikes, she stopped. My body relaxed. Nevertheless, the spanking hurt and left big red welts. The belt drove the lesson home. After I vowed to be a good girl, it was the last and only time my mother spanked me.

I wished I'd gone to the woods that day. But, on that beautiful, sunny morning, I had no clue it would end in catastrophe. I never found out what happened with the flooded barn. I didn't dare go back to look. And I could only play by myself from then on.

Only a child, I was already learning how to stay out of trouble and avoid punishment. Fear and unsafety built my inner foundation, squelching the natural desires I possessed. All I had to do was behave and not speak. I was safe by keeping myself out of the way. Therefore, I adapted well to being alone.

Now I know how to survive in the world: Don't make waves, keep to myself.

My Vow of Invisibility

This story is about more than a little girl growing up in a series of old rundown houses and a tale of her and her feisty friend's escapades. The childhood I experienced tells a blocked and denied energy biography. My 5th Chakra only received a trickle of that energy—I could barely speak. My throat remained closed except for the crucial moments at school and home. Falling silent, I grew more afraid. Throughout my life, everything I did—and didn't do—was based on a subconscious, programmed belief that I was too small and weak.

I'd made an unconscious vow of invisibility. Even though I wanted to be seen and heard, my survival instinct said, "No, lay low and stay quiet." Now I see what I couldn't have known then. My four lower chakras were blocked. The closed 5th Chakra demonstrated my weak foundation.

These days I'm stronger. However, someone can look at me funny, and my body reacts. I struggle with being triggered into fear. Often, in conversation with others, I appear to be okay. However, on the inside, my inner child cowers in fear. Her chest and throat tighten. A comment or look may be innocent. However, this part of me sees a bully or critic, and I need to hide.

Ordinary, everyday conversations can cause my heart to race. And out of the blue, my eyes start to tear up. I'm embarrassed and feel like an idiot. Then, I cover up with a fib. For example, I dab the corner of my eye and say, "I don't know why my eyes are watering today."

The older I got, the more my body reacted to my self-imposed invisibility. For years it sent me signals. I ignored them. So, my body tried harder to get my attention, and I succumbed to chronic throat and sinus infections, culminating in acute bronchitis. Then I stopped and listened.

The Mezzanine

We've reached the Mezzanine overlooking the Great Room. In today's world, our homes don't need a particular spot for a phone line. Nor do we require an exclusive desk for letter writing. Today, cell phones in our pockets allow us to create and communicate with ease. Yet, in this part of The House of You, we still establish a space to expand our creativity, self-expression, and listening skills. At this level, we're within an ear's reach of the upper and lower levels. And we have the perfect vantage point to see how energy in one part of our virtual house affects the rest of it.

The 5th Chakra (Throat Chakra) sits above our hearts in our physical bodies. Our Throat Chakra energy drives our expression, creativity, communication, and listening skills. It establishes our foundation to speak and be heard.

Renowned chakra expert, Anodea Judith, calls the 5th Chakra the gateway between our inner and outer world. Words are the vehicle for conveying what's happening inside us to the world outside us. The Throat Chakra permits the link between other people and us to share our thoughts and ideas. This chakra also connects messages between the mind, body, and spirit. The outer world we take into ourselves with the 2nd Chakra engages with what we send out from the 5th Chakra.

Hang in there; I know this concept is profound. Recall how empowerment energy flows upward from Mother Earth, starting with the Root Chakra to the Heart Chakra. Now we're entering the upper chakras of our inner home, where manifestation energy from Source flows downward from the Crown Chakra to the Heart Chakra.

Clearing our 4th Chakra brings down the walls around it. Love and understanding melt away our armor. Then, empowerment energy rises and allows us to speak our truth through the Throat Chakra. And even though this chapter is about an upper chakra, guess what— we're still going to be revisiting the lower chakras. A struggle in the upper chakras means a block in one or more of the lower chakras.

Did you notice my almost-voiceless behaviors in the story that opens this chapter? Not being seen and heard indicates a block in the 2nd Chakra. And at the 1st Chakra, I mastered my go-to survival pattern. To feel safe, I donned the cloak of invisibility at a very young age. Adults told me I was too shy and tiny for my age. Believing it, I played along. Staying out of the way as far as possible, I kept myself small and quiet. However, you've also seen the story that opens this book when I had no choice other than to take charge. There was only me. My vocal cords broke free when I screamed for help in those early morning hours. I expressed my voice in a new way as energy from my unblocked lower chakras traveled to my energy-starved Throat Chakra.

Congested Mezzanine – Blocked 5th Chakra
Disempowering, negative impact: quiet, loud, gossiping, secretive, poor listener, non-expressive

Throughout this chakra journey, we grow new perspectives on our current and past experiences. For example, breakthroughs in our energy system reveal how blocks in the upper chakras correspond to those in the lower chakras.

Imagine being upstairs in your house and you hear a noise from below. In an instant, your mind goes on alert. You've got to check it out. What if the water heater's about to blow? What if someone's trying to break in? Or maybe it's a mouse rummaging in those stuffed boxes.

Now imagine a blocked 5th Chakra. Residual fear and unexpressed emotions create a backlog of stored energy lodged in the throat. The pressure builds as it waits for a chance to escape. Do you ever get a lump in your throat? You are speechless, with a build-up of stuck emotion. Then we can't share our inner self with the outer world. Well, not until something triggers us, and we lose control. At that point, the emotion often bursts out of us sideways, uncontrolled.

When you look for the signs of a blocked Throat Chakra, you see them in yourself and others. To detect blocks in this chakra, listen for tone of voice. For example, one person can sound robotic, talking from their headspace, while another might speak with a high-pitched, childlike voice. You may notice both are avoiding their feelings. Not wanting to feel the pent-up emotions, they deny any sensations in their bodies.

We're afraid to be direct and deny chances to speak our truth. Then our words come out as criticism or condescension. And in cases such as mine, an inability to talk about our feelings can lead to passive aggressive behavior.

A myriad of times, I wanted to express my truth to my husband, Dennis. As I've noted, my throat often constricted, and my chest tightened. Trying to say what was on my mind, the words wouldn't come, and I'd only break down in tears. I often felt as if I couldn't hold in one more thing, or I would burst. Disappointment, tears, anger, fear, and anxiety would build up. Yet, I couldn't muster the courage to talk about how I felt until the feelings and emotions would finally spill out—blown out of proportion. Then, instead of crying, I'd meet Dennis' anger with an explosion of pent-up rage that I couldn't contain.

Our 5th Chakra dispels excess energy with outbursts of anger or tears. That's how it runs the show with negative emotions to relieve the pressure; we're not in charge of how that happens. However, I lived with the consequences of remaining in my self-imposed silent prison of fear for years.

A voice you've met before also appears in the blocked 5th Chakra, the inner critic. It loves to take charge, preventing us from expressing our authentic selves because of buried wounds in our lower four chakras. Our inner critic grew up hearing adults say, "Don't you dare talk back. Shut up, sit down, and behave." Excessive control and criticism continue to stifle our creativity and self-expression. In some homes, these rules were more stringent when addictive personalities or abusive behaviors were present. In this state, we withdraw into ourselves. And our inner child recites the mantra, "Never talk, never trust, never feel."

Meanwhile, we talk to ourselves all the time. Yet we're often unconscious of our internal conversations' effect on us. Awareness of our inner voices is crucial for our authentic truth to come through.

When we pay attention to the negative voices in our heads, we hear the voice of our frightened inner child. And we recognize the constant nag, the inner critic. The voice we hear may be a parent, teacher, religious leader, or an echo of someone else from our past. And, just as we did in the lower chakra work, we must stop, take a breath, and ask ourselves, "Who am I listening to?"

Even into adulthood, we still listen to the voices of authority we grew up with telling us, "No, no, no." And then, the energy charge gets caught in our throats when we try to get our words out. As a result, with only a trickle of it seeping through, many of us still only say what's appropriate and acceptable and keep the rest to ourselves.

Landing Swept Clean – Unblocked 5th Chakra
Empowering, positive effect: expressiveness, honesty, trustworthiness

An intuitive business coach once told me, "There's something you need to get off your chest. You're holding things in, and you must let them out." Considering my husband's mental and physical decline at the time, I understood the advice. Yet it took many years for me to begin to voice the fear and anxiety inside me. What that coach said was right. Holding everything in threw my energy centers out of balance. My self-prophesy came true. I was too weak. With no strength in my core, my inner truth stayed unspoken. And for sure, I couldn't yet tell anyone about my husband's issues, his consequent addictions, nor my anxiety—until I unblocked my Throat Chakra.

This open mezzanine floor plan allows communication between the upper and lower levels of the house. With an unblocked 5th Chakra, a wave of energy allows our inner truth to flow through our throats with ease. And we connect with another inner voice of our 7th Chakra—our Higher Self (the soul). As we clear away energy blocks across all the chakras, we become open to asking for and receiving true manifestation.

Our courage doesn't falter. Even if we feel scared, we remain grounded and centered during challenging conversations. We can stand up for what is rightfully ours, our innate worth. Speaking with our authentic voice, we shine without guilt. You may see how speaking your truth feels when reflected in the following story showcasing the power of an unblocked 5th Chakra.

Coffee with Rosa

My friend and client, Rosa, was working on manifesting prosperity. We created an outrageous goal for her—maximum dollars in minimal hours, and she loved the possibility. However, Rosa knew about the internal money blocks she needed to clear to transform her life as she envisioned was possible.

We started the Zoom coaching session with a guided visualization. First, I asked Rosa to close her eyes and imagine herself on a stage before an audience of friends, family, and colleagues. Among them are former teachers, classmates, coworkers, old bosses, exes, and other possible skeptics.

"I'm there," Rosa said. "I feel good. I'm comfortable on stage."

I said, "Good! Now you're carrying a huge sign. Printed on it, in large numbers, is your big income goal. Under that is the number of hours you work earning that money."

She raised her eyebrows and nodded.

"Walk to the front of the stage," I said. "Raise the sign high over your head, showing it to everyone."

I was surprised when she raised her arms. *She's getting it.*

Then I added the finale. "Shout loud with enthusiasm, 'I'm awesome at what I do! I make this much money. And I only work these many hours!'"

A half-smile crossed her face. "I'm awesome at what I do! I make this much money. And I only work these many hours!"

"Okay, Rosa, take a breath and tell me what just happened."

She took a deep breath and described the scene. "People are clapping and cheering me on."

"That's great," I acknowledged. "Your fans are supportive. What about the skeptics?"

She shook her head. "They're shooting me disapproving looks and laughing at me. Jeering and heckling. Somebody said, 'Get outta here.'"

I grinned, hearing, "Get outta here," in her upper western New York accent. Then, leaning in, I asked, "What else are they doing?"

"They're making fun of me, whispering, talking about me, and turning away," she said. "One woman said, 'Wouldn't that be nice. I should be so lucky.' And a couple of people got up and walked out."

"Take another breath, Rosa," I said. "Stay in the moment, taking it in. Now, start tapping on your collarbone point. And tell me how you feel after declaring your worth."

Rosa tapped and expressed the emotions and feelings of rejection rising in her. "I wish I wouldn't have shared that," she declared. "I feel defensive. My feelings are hurt. I'm scared. I'm embarrassed and exposed. They think I'm a fraud. What was I thinking? Some of the audience was brutal; I didn't prepare for that. I feel anxious, defeated, and resentful. I can't even speak now, and my throat is on fire. It's too much. I'm too much." She sighed.

I felt she had more feelings to share, so we continued tapping.

Rosa took another breath and said, "Why can't I be like the women who work less and earn big money? I have skills and experience. And the worst thing is, nobody gets to see my potential." She frowned. "I pull back, never crossing the finish line. I tell myself, 'Don't get your hopes up.'"

After a round of tapping on her feelings of disappointment and unworthiness, Rosa was ready for the next layer we would peel back.

"Take another breath and look at the picture again. How does the audience look now, Rosa?"

"It's better," Rosa said. "They're more curious and want to know more. And they're looking straight at me. A skeptic showed up, and one of my supporters escorted him out. No one looked at him. He can't stop me now." She outlined every detail of the positive shift in her audience.

Once Rosa saw a receptive crowd, I guided her to return to the stage and face them again.

I said, "Imagine a bright golden light entering your body through your Crown Chakra. The light fills you, and you glow from within. Extend your arms out, sending light to everyone. Watch as each of them is now glowing with this light. You're allowing them to shine their light as you shine yours."

Rosa sat up taller. "I feel lighter, more excited. I feel my passion again. I can do this."

"Put your hand on your heart and feel your inner power. The audience you pictured represents your subconscious mind. The negative reactions are your limiting beliefs. They are how and why you can or can't declare your worth and speak your truth."

We discussed how the skeptics were giving voice to her inner critic. When she listened to that voice, Rosa saw how she judged and beat herself up. These words were nothing more than old *misbeliefs* from old wounds. And we shifted that image of the naysayers with tapping. By changing the narrative running in our minds, we can change our perspective and transform our lives.

The next time we met on Zoom, I could see the steam wafting from her signature coffee mug in her hand. Rosa was jubilant. "It dawned on me, Sandy," she said. "I'm a coach. So, I've been walking around my house saying, 'I'm Coach Rosa.'"

Coach Rosa's 5th Chakra cleared. She's stepped up in a big way, no longer playing small. As a master trainer and coach, Rosa published her book, *Mind Over Platter.* Now she's the training and workshop coordinator for the company where she works. Rosa also has a growing group membership program and is a frequent podcast guest. She's blowing me away with *Coffee with Coach Rosa* featuring her live videos and her new podcast by the same name.

Rosa gained insight into how the negative comments from her imagined audience reflected her self-judgment and criticism. The shadow, her inner critic, lied, saying she was unworthy. She didn't have to believe it anymore. Finding her truth, Rosa's Throat Chakra cleared, and everything changed.

Shadow Power – From Lies to Truth and Open Self-Expression

Our inner voices show up in the way we speak to others. These communication styles develop when we're young. Therefore, any shadows we uncover in the Throat Chakra connect to those below in the 1st and 2nd Chakras.

For instance, shadows of fear and unsafety in our foundation, the Root Chakra, create weaknesses in the Throat Chakra. Some of us would cower in a corner or run. *It's safer to stay quiet and out of the way.* This part of us remains scared, depleting our energy and triggering us into silence. The inner child yearns for others to notice them. However, the shadows tell us it's not safe to speak. We shrink back, preferring to be safe than heard and understood.

On the other hand, some kids refused to stay tight-lipped. Their words often got them into trouble. Acting up was the only way to receive attention. Now in adulthood, they despise vulnerability and weakness. Vowing never to be vulnerable, they tend to talk over others and dominate conversations. They're brilliant at circumventing their emotions and feelings. These people have the loudest voices in the room, prone to sudden outbursts and swift reactions. They may yearn for calm while their shadow can't allow it. This shadow play is from the 1st and 2nd chakras.

These unconscious shadow behaviors from the lower chakras signal an imbalanced or blocked 5th Chakra. Whether quiet or boisterous, we listen to fear and our inner critic. The words we hear sound wise and valid. However, their clever little lies trick us into believing false wisdom. They're not keeping us safe. They're keeping us stuck.

We find our voice when our Throat Chakra shadow gets to speak. Once the shadow feels heard, we are more open to listening to others. And we embrace communication, speaking, writing, and creating with our authentic inner truth.

A Crowded Mind . . . Can Not Listen
—Ray Justice, *Ideas to Wonder*

Message from the Mezzanine

I am the connector, the landing, the gateway between your metaphorical inner house's upper and lower floors. Often, your stuff accumulates from both levels, blocking all the rooms throughout The House of You. And you get stuck here in the middle.

I represent your 5th Chakra, connecting your lower self with your Higher Self, integrating your ego and soul. Like a staircase cluttered with a backlog of stuff, emotional blocks can clog your Throat Chakra.

Do you struggle with speaking, writing, creating, or listening and hearing? They are all signs of blockage in your lower chakras. Investigating blocks and uncovering the shadows in your lower chakras helps the energy flow to your Throat Chakra. You can restore your innate communication and creative skills that the shadows distorted. Then you are free to express your authentic self.

To unblock your Throat Chakra, you have a tapping and journaling homeplay exercise in Chapter Eight of *Your Woo Woo Way Playbook*. You even get to make some fun noises. Your authentic self comes through in your voice and the words you choose with the Phone Home and Ignite Your Creativity homeplay.

The next chapter brings us to the attic where our 6th Chakra, the Third Eye, resides. It's the spot many of us are waiting for, where we see with our inner eyes and engage our intuitive imagination.

5th Chakra, Message from the Mezzanine
https://youtu.be/fpg1cjsiH9Y

SCAN ME

Chapter Nine

The Attic

The 6th Chakra – Wishful Thinking

1999, Keller, Georgia

*O**h God, I think I'm gonna be sick. I had no idea it was this bad.*

I was in a salon I call "Island Style," where I would be "renting a chair" for a few days a month. Before receiving a client, I needed to scrub under my styling station at years of dirt and hair clippings glued together with layers of lacquer hairspray. As I sprayed and wiped, the debris grew into a gunky mass of slime. Picture this scene: me, down on my hands and knees, with my butt sticking out from underneath the station. I started coughing from the ammonia fumes that made my eyes sting. Then bam! Trying to back out, I hit my head.

Ouch. Damn, that hurt. How does this place pass inspection? And what on earth have I gotten myself into now?

Searching for more cleaning tools, I followed the smell of burnt day-old coffee. Most salons have a multipurpose room stocked with hair color and other supplies. As soon as I opened the door to the back room, suffocating heat hit me in the face. A microwave sat on top of a refrigerator next to a stacked washing machine and dryer. Thick wads of towel lint were strewn all across the floor. The dryer door appeared to be growing a beard.

That's a fire waiting to happen.

Then I saw two young stylists seated at a tiny table nibbling on their sandwiches.

Oh wow, they're eating in here.

They paused mid-bite, looked at me, and didn't say a word. Dense negative energy and thick layers of dust engulfed the room. My subconscious judgment met their defensiveness. The message was quite clear: this salon was their home. They didn't want some highfalutin' big city stylist intruding on their territory. Flashing a nervous smile, I nodded and walked out of the room.

The voices in my head kept chattering.

This idea is gonna be more challenging than I thought. It's fine. I can make it work. They might come around.

That salon experience hit me hard. I was on a discovery mission to see if I wanted to live in Savannah, Georgia. It was a hair-brained idea. I could leave a lucrative career, start over in another state, and build a loyal clientele again. It was the perfect transition plan. All I needed was a place that would let me rent a chair to do hair for two or three days a month.

Accustomed to working in a higher caliber salon, I trusted that my work spoke for itself. And I set out to establish a foothold in the

Savannah area without worrying about where I worked. Denying the warning signs, I settled on a less-than-desirable location.

I was so wrong about this place. What am I going to do now?

Crestfallen, I flew back to our home in Virginia and faced my husband, Dennis, with trepidation. It was a disappointing excursion. I knew how he'd respond. He wasn't on board with my idea of uprooting us in the first place.

"When are you ever going to learn?" he asked. "You wanted it so bad you didn't even notice the red flags."

"I know. You're right," I said. My eyes stung with tears, and I willed myself not to cry—at least not right then. "I thought it would be okay, though."

Dennis was logical and pragmatic. I, however, looked at life through rose-colored glasses. We were at an impasse, and no comfort would come from him. Meanwhile, I had only shared half the truth. Dennis thought the move was about choosing a place where we could work and later retire. However, I left out the part about my desperation to remove us from the escalating, toxic environment. In my naivete, I believed that he could become clean and sober if we left behind his drinking buddies and easy access to drugs. I felt as if he was drowning and taking me down with him. And I clung to a lifeboat called "Savannah."

"That's how you always do things," he admonished. "You just jump right in thinking everything will turn out fine."

I felt the sting of his ridicule as Dennis prattled on about everything wrong with my so-called transition plan that dumbfounded him. I had no words to debate his premise that I had made a poor new salon choice.

Although Dennis could be negative, he was my biggest fan and best public relations guy; almost every week, someone would come to the salon and tell me they heard him rave about my work. He didn't understand why I would uproot my career, and he hated the idea of moving. Nonetheless, he acquiesced.

"You've followed me everywhere," he said. Then he paused. "It's your turn. Let's see how it goes."

Relieved, I thanked him for getting on board.

The following month, I returned to Island Style prepared to tell the owner I was quitting. It wasn't a good fit for me. She fired me first, though. "This isn't working out. Make this your last day," she sneered. I felt like she was talking to a delinquent teenager. Whatever else she said, I tuned it out.

I smiled. "I understand. Let me get my things," I said. And out the door I went, relieved yet feeling a tiny ping of rejection stinging my heart.

Gazing at the clear blue sky overhead, I took a deep breath and shook it off.

Keep going, Sandy. You can do this, and the energy was all wrong, anyway. It wasn't where you belonged.

I needed to open my eyes to greater possibilities. If I'd known I had a blocked 6th Chakra, envisioning my future could have worked better. As with most of my stories, I was unaware of my body's inner energy system. Instead, I was on a fool's errand, daydreaming about the future and still looking at the past—unable to see the whole picture.

When I tried to imagine my ideal life into being, I forgot to look out to the horizon. Instead, in typical fashion, I donned my big, rosy glasses and dove right in, never checking for hidden obstacles. In complete denial, I imagined an idyllic romantic ending. I'd close my eyes and picture my husband accepting treatment and embracing sobriety. I had no doubt I could change the trajectory of our lives.

Instead, our problems intensified. Finally, after going back and forth exploring options, we both got jobs in Savannah and made the move. However, I was still drowning in tears, heartbreak, and self-pity, and when I tried to meditate, the picture was blank and dark. Soon I would learn to unblock my 6th Chakra and discover the limitlessness of a clear Third Eye Chakra vantage point.

The Attic

Climb upstairs with me as we continue the tour of our virtual renovation house. We're entering the attic, the seat of our intuition, our 6th Chakra, or the Third Eye Chakra. The architect designed a cozy, imaginative, and creative space for us. There's even more room for storage. Consider this a Bonus Room, the perfect place for introspection, contemplation, and visioning.

In the 6th Chakra, we develop a more ethereal sense of mind and spirit. Often thought of as the sixth sense, intuition and imagination grow. While discovering exciting concepts and ideas different from our own, we start thinking for ourselves.

Excess Baggage in the Attic – Blocked 6th Chakra
Disempowering, negative impact:
lack of focus and judgment, obsessive, delusional, poor imagination

At any given moment, our bonus room in the attic space may not be as quiet as we thought—unrelenting, negative, inner head-chatter cuts through the silence. Alone with our thoughts, we're trapped in arguments with ourselves.

The light up here becomes blocked by a stack of crumbling cardboard boxes shoved against the window to the outer world. Sealed tight inside are not-so-great experiences and echoes of wounds in the lower chakras. We sit amid the dusty relics of our past. Remember the stuff we found in the basement? We gave these boxes new labels and elevated them to upper-level status.

Nevertheless, they hold those same unaddressed negative issues, bursting at the seams for attention. Everywhere we go, we've shlepped them with us. They're often too painful to look at, yet we can't let them go. Therefore, deep in the stuffy, angst-filled attic, we discover a new meaning for the word "shadowbox."

Even masters of personal development sometimes get stuck focusing on the 6th and 7th Chakras. That's because a blocked Third Eye Chakra can send us in all directions in pursuit of happiness and fulfillment, so we *feel* like we're making progress. Meanwhile, unless we clear our lower chakras, we bypass the transformation fuel and remain stuck.

When the 6th Chakra is blocked, we run on low energy, which can cause internal blindness. Our memory, vision, and imagination weaken. Constant thoughts spin in our heads, yet there's a diminished capacity for rationale. As in my Savannah story, we may hold a vision that makes us blind to everything else. Denial of negative emotions and feelings causes an energy imbalance. Then our bodies manifest headaches, vision problems, and vertigo.

Valuable energy trapped in lower chakras distorts our perspective and clogs the 6th Chakra with wishful thinking. As a result, our untethered minds turn to fantasies, delusions, and conspiracies. On the other hand, a blocked Third Eye Chakra can mean that our heads are in the clouds. Therefore, we're not grounded because the lower chakras suck up excessive energy. Then manifestation capacity becomes limited. We're ungrounded, and accessing our deep emotions feels unsafe. Our view of possibility narrows when only a trickle of energy gets through.

A classic example is a young woman fantasizing about having a big, elaborate wedding. Except she's only known her prospective partner for a short time. She pushes down any negative thoughts of red flags. Or somebody boasts about how they're going to make lots of money. Yet, they squander money on playing the lottery and can't pay their rent.

Becoming cynical, we're unable to picture a better life. The Third Eye energy center shuts down, blocking access to imagination, intuition, and visualization capabilities. Some of us also detach from our bodies while denying our feelings.

A 6th Chakra blockage limits access to our intuition. And we compensate by using rational thought, making us appear insensitive to others' feelings, emotions, and moods. Or, as Anodea Judith notes, we're "head-blind." How many times have we been head-blind in our own stories? Failing to trust our intuitive insights and gut instincts, we second-guess ourselves into another mistake. After the dust from the chaos in my personal life settled, I had to acknowledge I was oblivious to anyone's struggle except mine. Caught up in my mess, I couldn't see what even the people closest to me were going through.

Like other chakras, the 6th Chakra can shut down to protect us from troubling past events. However, pushing painful memories down takes a lot of energy. As a result, our overall memory becomes weak. We have trouble imagining changes in our lives and can't picture ourselves behaving otherwise, so we feel stuck in a situation. The Third Eye Chakra is depleted, cut off from vital energy. Looking back, I see how my husband's resistance to moving reflected his inability to envision a different and possibly better life.

Some of us may become spiritually closed-minded. We tend to stay with what's familiar. It doesn't feel safe to venture outside the tenets and teachings of our upbringing. This fear has been with us since the dawn of humankind, the ultimate fight, flight, or freeze response. If we left our tribe, we would be killed and eaten. However, when we can approach different ideas with an open 6ᵗʰ Chakra, a whole new world comes into view.

A Clear View – Unblocked 6ᵗʰ Chakra
Empowering, positive effect:
intuitive, imaginative, faithful, clarity of thought

There's a beautiful cedar chest filled with happy memories and interesting, inspirational ideas in our virtual attic. An open 6ᵗʰ Chakra provides energy to develop our imagination, vision, and personal identities.

We perceive the outer world with our physical eyes. And our Third Eye Chakra projects inner vision and perception on the movie screen of our minds. There we store reels of memories intertwined with fantasy, replays of daily activities, and dreams. From our inner movie content, we derive meaning. Then, these meanings arise in our conscious minds. Internal reflection leads to self-knowledge and balanced wholeness.

An open 6ᵗʰ Chakra activates our intuition born in the 2ⁿᵈ Chakra, where we feel those inherent gut instincts. Ideas and insights come to life, and information flows with an active imagination. As the 6ᵗʰ Chakra sees the way, we learn to recognize patterns. Our energy spikes, and creative sparks fly. We're in the proverbial "zone." With a well-balanced 6ᵗʰ Chakra, we stay calm and see events clearly as neutral observers. Fear and resistance from our lower selves don't cloud our perspectives. And an overarching vision brings meaning to our lives.

An Unsafe Mission
December 2019, somewhere in the Middle East

"I don't know. I don't think I can feel anything," Leila said. Though her camera was off, I could sense Leila concentrating. She sighed. "I'm not sure."

By most standards in her culture, Leila was an ordinary young woman. She attended university before starting a small coaching practice. And when her parents needed help, she complied without complaint. During holy days, Leila loved assisting in the cooking and preparation of elaborate dinner parties. However, she was striving to do extraordinary things beneath a shroud of secrecy. Leila wanted to grow her transformational coaching business and increase her income, and I committed to helping her succeed.

"Sandy, I've tried everything—books, classes, and workshops. Yet, there's no progress in sight," Leila said. "Something's blocking me from fulfilling my dreams. I just can't see it yet."

Leila fascinated me. It wasn't her problems that intrigued me. Most of my clients had similar issues. It had to do with Leila living in the Middle East. Working with me could bring her harm or even threaten her life. She opted to stay off-camera, and I promised to send each session's audio recording. I realized on the first call that there was more to it than time zones and schedules to her off-camera request.

"Leila, could you speak a bit louder, please? I'm having trouble hearing you," I said. Leila followed my lead in the tapping round, speaking just above a whisper. I turned up my volume and leaned in. Then, suddenly, it hit me.

Oh, my God. I think she's hiding in a closet.

She was risking everything. She lived in a war-torn country with threats of danger outside her door. At first, she struggled to feel any sensations in her body. Always surviving on her wits, it didn't feel safe to be in her body. However, Leila was determined to do the work. She trusted the process. In each session, I coaxed her out of her busy mind and into her body. Leila had an overenergized 6th Chakra that served her well in her life-or-death circumstances. However, she couldn't fulfill her mission or accomplish her vision. She needed to break through the blocks buried deep within her lower chakras.

While I regard coaching with reverence, working with Leila seemed even more sacred. Because of an unstable Root Chakra, she never felt safe. Leila lived on the epitome of shaky ground. During a visualization, she revealed that her parents survived an intense, devastating bomb attack. Leila was born into the energy of their terror. Their rigid religious beliefs and desperate need to protect her squelched her creative spark.

While driven to do great things, fear and anxiety caused Leila to retreat into her brilliant mind and vivid imagination. I began helping her get grounded and feel safe (1st Chakra), perhaps for the first time. Then, she rediscovered her inner child, who spoke of her long-forgotten deepest desires (2nd Chakra). Her inner wild child let loose with unbridled power and fury at the injustices of her life. Leila strengthened her core and her ability to act on her own behalf (3rd Chakra).

Bucking her culture and religion, she somehow avoided an arranged marriage. More than just evading a marriage, Leila didn't want to marry because she was in a secretive, committed relationship, which was a brave move. I felt impressed by her courage and fearful for her safety. And as if that wasn't enough, her outside world was literally exploding. The next wave of bomb-loaded rockets landed dangerously close to Leila and her family.

"Leila, are you doing okay?" I asked as we started our next call. "You're making phenomenal progress. However, I'm also worried about you."

"I'm good, Sandy. I avoid thinking about war. Bombs are a part of life," she answered. "I'm ready to shout out who I am and what I do to the world."

I gulped. "Wow, Leila, that's incredible." She was so new at facing her inner dark side. I wondered if she was ready.

"I'm planning to expand my business. I want to find a larger space to incorporate group activities," Leila said.

I felt Leila's complete joy. Yet I still feared for her safety. She was a walking, talking contradiction to the mores of her culture.

Is Leila still wandering in fantasyland? Can she survive?

However, Leila was diligent with the work. I witnessed her transformation as I guided her through the remaining sessions. Every week, we uncovered, cleared, and healed another block hidden deep within her subconscious. When Leila acknowledged her shadows and brought them into the light, she found the beautiful gift of clarity. She continued tapping as she created her business using her brilliant mind. She stayed grounded, no longer anxious and afraid. Practical and creative visualizations replaced Leila's fantasies.

Leila arrived on our final call full of confidence. "Sandy, your coaching is the most powerful process," she said. "I'm so glad to be not stuck in fear anymore."

"Wonderful, Leila. You've worked hard for your success, and it shows."

"I feel way more confident." Leila paused. "And I've already doubled my income!"

"Yes!" I shouted, arms in the air. "And while I showed you the way, you did the difficult part. I'm grateful for this opportunity to guide you and watch you shine."

She laughed. "Now I get to coach other women to reclaim their power and befriend their shadows."

Shadow Power – From Illusion to Perception

Our entire energy system often operates through the voices of our lower chakra shadows. Thoughts get skewed by an inner gang fighting it out in our heads, exemplified by my story at the beginning of the chapter. The overwhelmed, poor me part just wanted out.

My inner rebel led the charge, shouting, *Don't tell me what to do. I'm going for it.*

And without a clear vision, I packed my troubles right alongside my belongings and wishful thinking.

To achieve happier results, it helps to look back at the lower chakras for clues about what's blocked. Remember: Our shadows are born out of childhood wounds and traumas. Therefore, to restore energy flow, we must ask ourselves where the power of inner sight and perception became blocked.

So many of us grew up in situations where what we saw didn't match what adults told us. Often, they invalidated our natural intuition, imagination, and psychic abilities. In Leila's story, she shows us how the shadow of denial can also emerge in scary environments filled with violence, such as war zones. While we instinctively avert our eyes from disturbing images in our outer world, the shadow closes our Third Eye when it perceives a threat to our inner world. This shadow often tries to protect us by blocking our view of reality.

The shadow then controls us, and we switch to autopilot. It's what I call wandering off to "Lala Land." Maybe we are driving somewhere when all of a sudden, we're arriving at our destination. And we feel dumbfounded because we don't remember the drive.

We sit behind the wheel for a second, thinking, *Oh, my God—how did I get here?*

For example, one time I took a mental vacation and missed an exit on the highway. The next one was across the state line. That lack of focus and attention can be dangerous.

Unrealistic optimism can seem safer than examining deep feelings and emotions. In my case, I tend to become Scarlett O'Hara in Margaret Mitchell's *Gone With The Wind.*

I can think about it tomorrow. Tomorrow's another day.

The 6th Chakra shadow can also cause people to adhere to a rigid belief system. They think there's only one right way. Anything outside of their limited point of view gets rejected as false. They don't play well with others who don't follow the same life principles.

Our Third Eye Chakra energy can also be excessive rather than depleted. The shadow with too much energy robs us of our ability to concentrate. The harder we try, the worse it gets. We can't think our way into thinking clearly, leading to obsession, delusions, nightmares, and hallucinations. Ever stall out when facing an important decision? An overwhelming flush of energy ignites our inner critic and her companions, self-doubt and confusion, leaving us bogged down in fear and "what if?" questions. Then our indecision creates an internal storm of guilt.

In my story from Chapter One, the cold, sterile emergency room slapped me back into reality. I found the Southeast's torrential rains symbolic. My husband and I were slipping yet again down a slippery slope. However, this time, EFT tapping threw me a lifeline. It held me steady, steering me through an onslaught of downturns and the innumerable decisions I had to make.

The shift from illusion to perception happens when we open the curtains. We find clarity when we bring our 6th Chakra shadows out of the dark and give them a voice. Then, with a clear vision to see beyond our struggles, we can look at things afresh.

This vantage point allows us to escape our daily lives for periods of introspection and self-actualization. Clearing the lower chakras to get here, we feel empowered to spend time in our virtual attic. Seeking clarity, we discover the solution to our dilemmas, opening us up to listen to the wisdom of our hearts. Then, we're free to visualize our desired future and make it *real*.

> Can you accept the notion that once you change
> your internal state, you don't need the external world
> to provide you with a reason to feel joy, gratitude,
> appreciation, or any other elevated emotion?
> —Joe Dispenza, *Breaking the Habit of Being Yourself:*
> *How to Lose Your Mind and Create a New One*

Notes from the Attic

I am your 6th Chakra, the Third Eye. In The House of You, I regulate your ability to see and perceive patterns in the world. I am considered the energy center of psychic sight. My primary purpose is to help you see all you are in the present moment.

When you're distracted by virtual reality and wishful thinking, I become blocked and can't function well. I relinquish control to your shadows. And you're ruled by wounds and negative beliefs in your lower chakras.

Clearing out the old boxes of misbeliefs that block your view allows you to regain equilibrium. In balance, you can see your life's purpose unfolding in front of you.

Your mind stays calm and allows you to see clearly. You become the observer and step back from or above your circumstances to gain a clearer perspective.

You now have a broader vision and a new worldview of your surroundings, other people, and the things affecting you. As a result, it becomes easier for you to make decisions and set intentions. You can step into action because you see the bigger picture.

What if your next tapping session reveals a great idea? It could. Check out the Tapping for Clarity homeplay in *Your Woo Woo Way Playbook*. Afterward, consider taking a nap and trust your inner self to guide your way.

An open Third Eye catches the bright sparks of awareness from our 7th Chakra, the Crown, the receptacle of Source Energy. Your dreams await you in the next chapter, where we reach the sacred portal to divine manifestation energy.

6th Chakra, Notes from the Attic
https://youtu.be/eXdjp5n1itQ

Chapter Ten

The Stargazer Deck

The 7th Chakra – My Catholic Brain

September, Lockport, New York, age six

"Now I lay me down to sleep, I pray the Lord, my soul to take," I recited. My knees were on the cold, wooden floor beside my bed, where I propped my elbows to fold my hands in prayer.

My mother stood over me, watching.

"Wait. Mom, what's God going to do with my soul?" I asked. I turned toward her, my body still in prayer position. "Is it like when somebody takes my picture, and they don't really take anything?"

My mother laughed, half snorting. "No, it means if something happens to you while you're sleeping, you go to Heaven. And the word is, *keep,* not *take.* Now stop with the questions and get to sleep. You gotta get up bright and early for school tomorrow."

If something happens to me?

I didn't sleep much. It wasn't only because I worried something could happen to me in the night. It was nervous excitement, something I now call "nervecited." The next day was big—my first day of Grade One at Saint Mary's School.

There were twenty-seven other children in my class. Our teachers were Sisters of Mercy Nuns. They got to work right away, showing us the proper way to pray—no more nursery rhyme prayers. We were in the big leagues. Every student in class got a kid-size Catechism. The little book contained everything we had to know about being good Catholics. We learned the ten commandments, the seven sacraments, three kinds of sin, and four places we might go when we die. And my six-year-old brain's wheels started turning.

Oh, that's how it works.

Praying to the Lord, "my soul to keep," meant we wouldn't go to Hell. Instead, we could go straight to Heaven. We could maybe even bypass Purgatory, God's waiting room. Aside from Limbo for unbaptized babies, Purgatory is where God sends us if our souls aren't ready for Heaven.

My mother covered all her bases too. She insisted my older siblings and I attend Catholic school. The nuns' strict rules of behavior *might* keep us in line. Mom loved the fourth commandment, "Honor Thy Father and Mother." She focused on the honoring part. If she and my dad fought, for instance, she'd pull out that darn commandment. I can still picture her bent over, one hand on her hip, wagging a finger at me. She'd say, "Remember, honor thy father and mother. What happens at home stays at home."

I wouldn't confess my sins in our church until the following year, when I turned seven. Yet my intuition warned me. My mother's punishment for disobedience outweighed any penance received in the confessional. I never questioned her rule, except in my mind. Talking back to her was never an option for me.

At church and school, every prayer began with the Sign of the Cross.

In the name of the Father, Son, and Holy Ghost.

That got my wheels spinning.

Ghost? Is that how He knows all and sees all? He's a ghost God?

Never opening my mouth, I held back a constant thread of questions. My silence kept me out of trouble. And I was already a master at staying quiet anyway. The last thing I needed was my mother's wrath for being too inquisitive in class. My classmates and I were good little Catholics. Thoroughly indoctrinated and devoted, we loved the church and its teachings.

My mom was right; I *did* receive an excellent education. The brilliant nuns taught us critical thinking, preparing us for college. However, we were required to accept and adhere to Catholicism's dogma without question. It would take me a few more years before I started thinking for myself and recognized my 7th Chakra's early stages of development.

There seems to be some residual Catholic muscle memory in me. It's an ingrained religious response. For instance, I have an automatic reflex if I hear the phrase "In the name of the Father," my right hand goes up, and I tap my forehead with my fingertips—executing the Sign of the Cross maneuver.

The first form of tapping might be the Sign of the Cross. Think of it—you tap on the Third Eye Chakra, then the Heart Chakra, ending with tapping each collarbone point.

My inner Catholic girl still loves the beauty of rosary beads. Now I see the rosary as a natural tapping tool. We tap the fingertip points while moving from one bead to the next. However, we dedicate fifty of those beads to reciting the Hail Mary prayer. Much to the nuns' chagrin in Catholic school, we acquired a unique talent to finish the rosary in record time. We were innocent of the irreverent way we said those sacred meditative prayers. These days, if I'm ever in a life-threatening situation, rapid-fire Hail Marys are guaranteed to spew out of me. Today's rappers got nothin' on me. And I add tapping for good measure.

All kidding aside, I spent years searching for the magic formula for success and fulfillment. Countless books, audio programs, and workshops helped me build a lucrative career. The beauty industry was good to me, and I loved every minute of it. Then a subtle yet intense yearning for spiritual expansion and happiness altered my focus. My body, mind, and spirit awakened as I turned inward to my core.

In one serendipitous moment, I received Nick Ortner's invitation to try tapping right when I was ready for it. With tapping, my anxious thoughts subsided long enough for me to hear the wisdom from my Higher Self. I knew I was going in the right direction and had work to do, following a path to clear my chakras. Along the way, my awareness shifted.

As we progress through the chakras, we access wisdom, understanding, and connection to Spirit.

Stargazer Deck

Come on up. The view is divine. We've reached the rooftop Stargazer Deck, the pinnacle of our inner renovation house. From this vantage point in the 7th Chakra, it feels like we can touch the sky. Yet we're still safe, anchored to the firm foundation. While the shadows voiced their fears during tapping sessions, our lower chakra blocks cleared. We let go of our attachments to negative emotions and misbeliefs. And the burdensome weight of past unconscious wounds has lifted. Seeing things from a higher perspective opens us to divine inspiration, wisdom, and understanding.

Closed Due to Inclement Weather – Blocked 7th Chakra

Disempowering, negative impact:
disconnected, ungrounded, lacking faith, no direction or purpose

We close the shutters and hunker down when the weather turns harsh, and storms approach. Power outages can leave us sitting in silence and darkness. Connections to others may be limited. While we crave access to the upper deck to glimpse what lies beyond our homes, we don't dare.

Likewise, emotional storms can block our Crown Chakras, impeding Universal Divine energy from entering our bodies. And we tend to forget about the divinity within us. Fear, doubt, and shame in our lower chakras fog our brains, constraining awareness.

Energy leaking from our lower chakras builds, becoming excessive in the 7th Chakra. Uncontained, it may seep out through the Crown Chakra. All the while, we tend to think that this power is *out there* somewhere. Untethered, we can get lost in space, reaching for connections with a higher power. As a result, our lofty ideas fail to land or make an impact.

Our 7th Chakra can be blocked from below as well. The manifestation energy comes down from Source and ideally flows to the Heart Chakra, where it unites with rising empowerment energy from the lower chakras. However, when our Heart Chakra is blocked, the heart hardens, and nothing gets through that barrier. Trapped excess energy in the Crown Chakra often causes our minds to spin in constant thought loops. We see endless possibilities of what we might manifest. However, there needs to be more clarity in choosing one idea to focus on and bring it forward.

Storm Clears – Unblocked 7th Chakra
Empowering, positive effect: higher consciousness, universal love, wisdom

The deck has opened. The storms have cleared, and clouds have dispersed. The sun, moon, planets, and stars are once again visible. When inner storms calm, our Crown Chakras clear, amplifying awareness. As our spiritual nature awakens, our connection to Spirit heightens. Embodying the divine light within us, we shine it out to the world. And as we become aware of our oneness with the Conscious Universe, we experience bliss. The enlightenment we seek no longer eludes us.

An open Crown Chakra is the portal to Source energy, where we conceive ideas and insights that move to the Third Eye Chakra, igniting our imagination and intuition. The energy continues, flowing into the Throat Chakra, allowing us to speak our truth. And as we embody enlightened consciousness, we complete the manifestation process. Trust in infinite possibilities brings our visions to reality. The amount of wisdom, self-knowledge, consciousness, and spiritual connection is limitless. It's as vast as the Cosmic Universe.

Now, my friends, affirmations can work. Energy flows into and through us with ease. All of our senses are alive, embracing the beauty of life.

Manifestation occurs when we reach for how it *feels*. First, we had to feel the not-so-good feelings to heal and clear them. When we unclog the dark messiness, space opens for positive emotions. Their positive vibrations attract more positivity. We're tuning in and raising our vibrations to meet our Higher Power. We set an intention. Then we embody the feeling of already having what we desire.

Holding this feeling, our affirmations signal to the Universe we're ready. Then we must release our attachment to the outcome. We end the affirmation or prayer by saying, "This or something better," allowing Spirit to fulfill our wildest dreams.

Anxious Eileen
Spring 2018, Washington, D.C.

"I don't know, Sandy. I'm having a hard time," said Eileen. She sounded weak and defeated.

"Oh gosh, what's going on, Eileen? You look tired," I said watching her on the screen with concern.

"I'm beat. My anxiety is worse," Eileen said, her eyes filling with tears. "And I'm completely drained by this constant depression."

"Oh, Eileen, I'm sorry you're going through this."

She sighed. "I'm praying you can help me get out of my spiral. And I'm afraid my husband's getting tired of me being this way."

We dove right in with a quick round of tapping, lowering the intensity of her angst.

During a previous session, Eileen recounted a devastating trauma. Her father died when she was only four years old. The cause went unexplained. She didn't understand why Daddy wasn't coming home. No one would answer her questions or give her any comfort. Instead, they told her to be a big girl and suck it up. She learned to deny her feelings. And throughout her life, Eileen battled intense nervousness and crushing sadness. Never feeling safe in her body, anxiety became Eileen's perpetual companion.

Now an adult, Eileen suffered the physical consequences of holding everything in for so long. A debilitative disease weakened her body, and her emotional problems ballooned. However, the medical and psychological help Eileen received didn't stick. And growing impatience from Eileen's husband heightened her anxiety. He was a kind and caring man. Nevertheless, he believed in self-control and self-reliance. Therefore, he didn't understand her "weaknesses."

After we tapped together, I asked her how she felt.

"Better, calmer," she replied.

"Excellent, Eileen, that's awesome," I exclaimed.

"Yes, thanks. I don't know how to maintain it, though." Eileen heaved a deep sigh. "I want it to last. Nothing else has worked to keep me balanced." She frowned. "Every day, I wake up with intense anxiety because I know I'm going to crash. By 4:00 p.m., heavy depression hits."

I nodded my head and put my hand on my heart.

Her tears fell like a dam overflowing. "I have no energy left. I can't attend Bible study. My sculpting projects sit collecting dust. I haven't even been able to go running." She paused and blotted her eyes with a tissue. "And that makes me even sadder."

I said, "I know, breaking through and feeling better doesn't seem possible. Notice how fast you shifted and relaxed just now, though."

Eileen nodded in agreement. Yet she still didn't believe she could sustain it.

"Okay, take a deep breath, Eileen. Let's go deeper. Come out of your busy mind," I instructed.

"Where does the anxiety sit in your body?"

Eyes closed, she raised her hands behind her head. "The back of my head is tense, not relaxed."

Finding the anxiety in her body was a good sign of progress. It helped me to know which chakras needed clearing. "Does this anxiety have a color, a shape? Is it an animal, an archetypal figure?"

"It's gray, a big gray blob," Eileen answered.

"Does it have a name?" I asked. "Is it *Anxious Amanda* or perhaps, *Frightened Fred?* And if it feels big, call it what it is, *Fear,*" I said, emphasizing the last word.

"Nelson," Eileen said. "I don't know why I know this. It's like the Full Nelson wrestling hold. It's got a hold on me and keeps me anxious and in my mind."

"Perfect, Eileen," I replied. "Take another breath and start tapping. You're going to dialogue with this shadow part of you called Nelson."

She repeated the words I gave her. "Hello, Nelson, there you are, where you've always been. Why won't you change?"

"Because I don't want to," said Nelson, whose commanding voice came from deep inside Eileen.

During the dialogue, Eileen expressed her frustration with Nelson, who had a tight hold and wouldn't let go. She saw how extreme anxiety and depression felt normal to her. And she didn't like it. Nelson was old, reliable, and even comfortable, and I could see it was time to confront the Full Nelson.

She repeated after me once again while tapping. "I'm tired and frustrated." "You have to change." "I know you want to protect me."

"You're using an old reptilian method." "It's not working." "We need a new way, my way."

We tapped and honored the years of protection Nelson provided. And she gave her anxiety shadow, Nelson, a new job.

"You don't have to go away. You can be my guardian angel, watching out for me," Eileen said, with peace washing over her face. "Let go of your hold on me," she said, continuing to tap. "When you want my attention, whisper in my ear." "Or tap me on the shoulder." "I promise to stop, tap, and ask what you want to tell me."

I asked my question once more. "How do you feel, Eileen? Did anything come up for you?"

"I saw two separate parts of me," Eileen said softly. "It explains so much." Her eyes flashed with a new brightness, and she sat up straighter. "Sometimes when I go out, I don't know what to do or how else to be. I've been anxious my whole life."

"Incredible, Eileen. What a huge breakthrough. I'm so excited for you," I said. Then I gave her some homeplay. "This awareness is new to the primitive part of your brain, your shadow. Here's a good practice for you. Before your feet hit the floor every morning, notice the thoughts in your head and whether anxiety is building. Then, tap and acknowledge the negative emotions. Express your fear, worries, and disappointments. Don't try to fix it. Instead, voice it and honor it—clear it."

"Aha," she exclaimed. Eileen flashed a grin. "We're in the 1st Chakra again, aren't we?"

"You're right," I said. "We've come full circle, back in the lower chakras to see what's hidden there. There are more layers and aspects to uncover. While working on the Crown Chakra, recall a timeless quote from the Bible, 'As above, so below.'"

"I hadn't thought of my chakras that way," said Eileen.

"The Crown Chakra is your portal to the Divine," I said. "Connection problems here stem from blocks in the lower chakras. We're inspecting for cracks in your foundation. You've held your anxiety and unsafe feelings for so long. And your shadow, Nelson, protects you, holding onto them even tighter. Keep tapping to release that tight grip."

"I'd love to find some peace," Eileen said. "I've worked so hard at this. And I pray to God for help."

"Of course, Eileen," I said with compassion. "Tapping doesn't take away from sacred prayers—it enhances them. You have the tools I've taught you. And you don't have to be scared all the time anymore." Then I gave her the second part of her homeplay to tap when she prays.

"Even in church?" she asked.

"Yes," I said. "Place your hand on your Heart Chakra at the breastbone. Then tap with your whole hand or fingertips. Or use one of the other techniques I showed you. I assure you, no one notices."

The point was for her to stay grounded and present to foster a clear connection with God. Prayer is an open channel. It anchors us in Mother Earth's grounding energy and meets Source energy in the Heart Chakra.

I added one more homeplay for her. "Whenever you feel anxious or depressed, tap and remind Nelson of his new job as your guardian angel. Tap and ask, 'What do I need to know?'"

The homeplay instructions were all Eileen needed to move beyond her fears. After that, prayer became a catalyst, reminding her to tap.

Following that final session, I received an email from Eileen. The subject line was a phrase I love hearing from my clients: *Sandy, you're never going to believe it.*

I'm feeling better than I have in years. I'm tapping. It quiets anxiety faster than a twenty-minute meditation. I feel energized, and I'm back to sculpting. And listen to this—I'm invited to showcase my work at a prestigious gallery here. Who would've thought? I'm elated and grateful.

And one more thing, my husband noticed the changes in me. We're closer than we've ever been. Best of all, it's not too woo woo at all. Tapping enhances my faith. I'm grateful for tapping and your coaching.

Blessings, Eileen

Her lifelong search for peace, love, and harmony came to fruition. Eileen transformed her body, mind, and spirit by unblocking her chakras. Today she has the tools to address her fears. Eileen taps whenever signs of anxiety, sadness, or self-doubt arise. As a result, she's living her best life—instead of dreaming about it. Eileen is grounded at the Root while opening to miracles through her 7th Chakra.

Shadow Power – From Attachment to Detachment

The thirst for knowledge increases throughout life as the 7th Chakra develops. It's natural for us humans to seek awareness and spiritual connection. Yet, we can be held back by a shadow of attachment. This shadow's fear is cemented firmly in the Root Chakra. Yet it comes up to the Crown Chakra. And we cling to what no longer serves us.

We left things unattended in our foundation. Therefore, the upper deck is unsteady. The 7th Chakra is blocked, and at the same time, we're afraid to go back down and release the attachment shadow.

Eileen's story exemplifies what happens when we feel unsafe as children. We give birth to shadows and create survival patterns. Yet stepping beyond our family paradigm seems unthinkable. We could be ostracized by them, our community, or the church. Or we may worry about what other people think of us. Unable to fight or take flight, we can only freeze. Then we're stuck between our earthly insecurities and our spiritual longings. The cycle continues. We feel pulled in all directions except where we'd be most happy.

And attachment to what no longer serves us often has a companion. Sharing its space in the Crown Chakra is dissociation. This shadow tells us not to look at unpleasantness. It's safer to disconnect. However, it gives us a false sense of control and only serves to alienate us from others. Then, we escape further into our minds. Our heads fill with more worrisome thoughts. More afraid than ever, we still don't feel safe. Our shadow runs the show.

Once again, it's key to remember our shadow's only job is protection. In her book, *The Energy Codes,* Dr. Sue Morter calls the shadow The Protective Personality. Acknowledging shadows is the best way to find the clarity we seek. On the other side of dissociation is the gift of detachment, which gives us the ability to step above our issues and become neutral observers. With this perspective, we see how our shadow has protected us. And we can clear away what's not working anymore. As a bonus, there's no need to trash our upbringing, schooling, or religion.

Detaching from what others think of us lets us be detectives—or inspectors in our virtual house. Shining a light in the dark through all our chakras, we discover what's holding us back. Meanwhile, as we clear the blocks away, the good parts remain in place, strengthened by free-flowing energy.

Another unique gift from our shadow of fear is grounding. Once anchored in safety instead of fear, we're free to ponder the greatness of the universe.

Your creative and manifesting mind is ready for something great.
—Ray Justice, *Ideas to Wonder*

Viewpoints from the Stargazer Deck

You made it. I've been waiting for you. I'm your 7th Chakra, where experiencing the state of grace is possible. Here you let go of earthly burdens, allowing you to observe life circumstances from a higher perspective.

You didn't feel safe in your body until you cleared this space. You visited your Crown Chakra only to escape fearful situations. Solutions to your struggles were elusive as you searched outside yourself instead of within.

For survival, you denied your emotions and depended on intelligence. Spending time in cerebral activity, you were often insensitive to other people's hardships.

From the top in the 7th Chakra, you might be unaware of or ignore any lower instability. Nevertheless, you must go back down and reinspect the lower levels. Shine a light in the darkness once more. And retrieve the keys to keeping your Crown Chakra open. They're held in the subconscious attachments hiding in your lower chakras. With those blocks cleared, you can stop overthinking and surrender to Spirit.

It's safe to let go of the thoughts, beliefs, and attitudes that cloud your mind. Your Crown Chakra opens to receive Source energy. And your shadows feel safe enough to let you linger. You can see the bigger picture with new awareness from this clear vantage point. You can trust in Spirit and infinite possibilities. Remaining grounded, you can also accept life on life's terms. In other words, while acknowledging that life happens, you're ready to handle whatever comes your way. And you can amplify creative elements of the universal life force in you.

Working with your Crown Chakra, we're going to add another layer to your tapping with the Meditation with Tapping homeplay in *Your Playbook*. Are you ready to let your Higher Self's wisdom abound?

In the final chapter, step back and see the entire renovated House of You. And examine your inner home as a living, breathing powerhouse of energy.

Notes from the Stargazer Deck
https://youtu.be/4uHhLKb-khc

Chapter Eleven

The House of You Complete

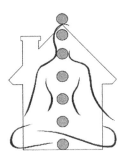

The Fear of Missing Out (FOMO)

June 2019, Rochester, New York

"**I** want to go," I whined. The words blurted out of me, uncontrolled. I'd turned into a four-year-old, curling up in a chair.

"I'm not leaving you," said my life partner, Ray, as he turned toward me. Baffled, he ran a hand through his hair and adjusted his glasses. "This is a special birthday trip from my kids—only me and them," he said. "And it's the only time they can be together without their spouses and kids."

My mind jolted back to reality. Embarrassed, I jumped up and took off for the shelter of my bathroom. Splashing ice-cold water on my face, I tried to reduce the redness and quell my tears. I looked up at the mirror and started tapping. "Oh my God, that was awful."

From my reflected image, my inner critic scolded, "Oh sure, *now* you tap."

My infantile outburst was preventable. I'd felt off-kilter for two days as if the air wasn't right. Yet, I denied my body's subtle signals. By the third day, the needy, nagging thoughts I kept ignoring intensified. When I couldn't contain them anymore, my inner child took over. Wanting to say what I couldn't, she felt abandoned, needing attention and acknowledgment.

"You could've tapped three days ago," I said, tapping and talking to the mirror. "You teach people how to do this. Practice what you preach already."

The tears slowed and stopped as I tapped through, berating myself and acknowledging my inner little one. I promised to pay more attention to her needs. It appeared that we had FOMO, an intense fear of missing out.

My inner child tantrum occurred because my life had turned upside down. My new-found, late-in-life relationship with a fantastic man, Ray, was beyond incredible. However, I hadn't quite adapted to my new home. The virtual cement on the foundation was still wet. It took me a while to see why. I'd spent my entire life living on shaky ground. Now I could learn to let go of fear and trust I was safe. I'm ever grateful for Ray. He gave me understanding, guidance, patience, and love. It was everything I needed to heal lingering grief and sadness.

My tearful outburst is an example of how the transformation journey can unfold. Remember—we must come to terms with the never-ending process. Every time something triggers us, there's an underlying negative emotion. It can often be the same one we've worked on before. There's another layer to peel away, another gift uncovered behind the pain.

I'd lost touch with one of the most important lessons I teach. Pressure builds under unexpressed emotion. If it's not released, it erupts on its own. And then, we're left to deal with consequences. Since the rude awakening of experiencing my inner child again in real time, I have helped my clients through similar episodes.

With renewed clarity, I paid close attention to my feelings and recognizable bodily sensations. I start to get over-sensitive, weepy, impatient, or defensive. And my uncensored inner critic talks out loud. That's when I know a long walk outside or soaking in a hot bath is in order. And tapping whenever an uncomfortable feeling comes up keeps me from imploding again. The key is awareness, catching the symptoms of triggers, and addressing them as soon as we notice them before they get out of hand. Next, we can tap for physical sensations and emotions, so keeping stress lowered and energy balanced becomes easier.

These days, I celebrate with my clients. Their ability to tune in to their bodies inspires me. When I ask them for celebrations, I hear, "I got mad. Then I tapped on it and just let it go."

Preparedness

A home renovation includes preparation for weather conditions and system breakdowns. Wherever we live, regardless of the climate, proper weatherizing protects us against the elements. Installing adequate insulation and seals around doors and windows is imperative. Maintaining indoor comfort levels when leaks are everywhere takes a lot of energy. And a damaged roof can cause problems throughout the house. Staying on top of home maintenance allows us to be ready for anything. In case of power outages, flashlights, batteries, candles, and lighters are necessities. If there's a fireplace, dry firewood must be available. And stocked cupboards sustain us when we're homebound.

Inevitable upheavals in our bodies, minds, and spirits also call for preparation. Now and then, we may experience what I call inner earthquakes. Our emotional reactions to external situations can shake us to our core. However, we're prepared for any circumstance with the potent mind-body tool, tapping. It keeps us steady throughout such stormy inner turbulence and never needs batteries. And by understanding the power held within our chakras, we can move through obstacles faster. Then, when things settle and the air clears, we're safe to carry on again.

Shadows Everywhere

Every year at the end of winter, in *every* house we lived in, my mother took down the heavy curtains used to prevent cold drafts. Then, she supervised as my sisters and I did the spring cleaning. We were astounded at what showed up when sunlight streamed through the windows.

I'm still awed by how much dust can accumulate underneath and on top of everything. And I'm always surprised by what else I find. Little treasures hidden under the couch, or a bed, emerge.

Hey, it's my favorite hair tie!

Shadows lurking in the dark are the same. And every area in our virtual house can harbor them. They clog the space until we pull back layers of old curtains and acknowledge their presence. It can be daunting to dust off boxes and sweep out the cobwebs. However, we reveal their gifts and strengths as we bring the shadows into the light.

Our inner beings' shadows, born out of past wounds, hide out in our lower chakras, remaining shrouded in darkness. Additionally, these tricky characters can wander into our upper chakras. Therefore, we must be on the lookout. Shadows try to get our attention by blocking one or more of our valuable energy centers.

For example, our vulnerable inner child may appear, and we can't speak our truth. This block is evident in the 5th Chakra when the Throat is blocked. We must return to the 2nd Chakra to find the original wound. By cleaning out the basement, we can practice speaking up. We're free of the inner child's scary environment. And while we're there, we can identify probable blocks in the other chakras.

My grandmother started a tradition when I was eight. Recognizing my mother's disinterest in housekeeping, she came to our rescue and helped us clean. Grandma put us girls to work scrubbing every inch of the house from top to bottom. I didn't think to ask why my brother didn't do any housework. Back then, society considered it "women's work." No one expected boys to help. That kind of thinking caused a lot of trouble when we Baby Boomers grew up and married.

When addressing our shadows, take a hint from my grandmother's house-cleaning technique. We can start at the top, in the Crown Chakra, and work down. However, sometimes the better approach is to begin at the Root Chakra. Then, move upward, one chakra at a time. Or we can pay attention to the part of us that hurts the most and investigate from there.

It's essential to remember how our shadows are birthed in chakras one through four, the Root to the Heart. If you're struggling with anything above them, ask your body to show you where to search for solutions. Your body never lies.

Susan Surrenders
During Hurricane season, North Carolina

Susan's attention drifted. Her voice echoed with panic as she said, "I'm sorry. I'm distracted. The wind's intense, and I'm afraid my tree out front might come down on the house."

"Okay, Susan, stay with me," I said, watching her image on the screen. "Put your hand on your heart. Let's tap to help you stay grounded and feel safe."

Susan had worked hard throughout our coaching sessions, which was paying off. Progress and positive changes were evident. Health and vitality replaced the wall of extra weight on her body. And she established her dream of a nonprofit foundation as her legacy. Yet, Susan's anxiety remained with hair-trigger panic attacks. Still, she committed to uncovering the deep-seated fears still hidden within her.

"As long as the connection is good, let's stay on the call," I said. "You told me you fortified your house against high winds and torrential rain. You battened down the hatches. Trust. Take a slow, easy breath. I've got you. You are safe."

Together we weathered the storm. Now and then, a loud cracking sound pierced the air. Tree limbs were breaking off, frightening Susan. I found it hard not to be afraid for her as the storm raged outside her door. However, after each wind-driven threat, I led her back to a feeling of safety. We talked and tapped, talked and tapped. During quiet, eerie lulls, Susan experienced divine aha moments of profound discovery. An active imagination process unleashed a long-forgotten childhood memory.

"Isn't that interesting? I never thought of it that way," she said, surprised. "I forgot all about that incident when I was six. There was a tropical storm, and the rain came fast and furious. I was with my four-year-old brother, and we couldn't make it to the house. Rushing into our neighbor's shed, I pushed my brother in first. As we huddled together inside, I couldn't console Tommy or stop his crying. My body grew tenser with each ear-piercing scream. Still, we held onto each other tightly without letting go."

"What a frightening scene, Susan," I exclaimed. "What happened?"

"The hellacious wind and pounding rain weren't the worst of it. When it was over, the real storm commenced. Our father found us asleep in the shed. I received severe punishment for not giving my brother proper protection. In my mind, my father only cared about Tommy. He didn't even ask if I was okay. Because my father saw girls as insignificant, I assumed all men felt the same. Now, almost sixty years later, I don't feel worthy of feeling safe, let alone loved."

"Okay, Susan," I said. "Whenever you feel anxious, put your hand on your heart. Then, ask yourself this simple yet valuable question. 'How old am I right now?'"

Susan laughed. "Oh, okay. That worked before with my food cravings. I asked that question whenever I opened the refrigerator or cupboard doors."

Susan and I ended our call when the sun came out at her place. She relaxed into a calm, safe state of mind. She gained a new understanding of her fears. I told her to be aware of her tendency to spin in worrisome thoughts and instead tune into her body.

I'm happy to report that Susan is quick to catch her fear-filled mind-chatter. She's learned that anxiety and nervousness are the same energy as excitement. Now she can harness that energy to propel herself into the life of her dreams. Embracing self-forgiveness allowed her self-compassion and self-worth to emerge.

No longer afraid of her inner darkness, Susan's light shines even brighter. Abundance grows in every aspect of her life. Relationships with her family have improved, and new friendships abound. Susan may still find things scary sometimes. However, she's open to what frightened her the most. Susan is ready to attract a loving relationship. She feels safe—willing to give and receive love.

Virtual Walkthrough – Complete

Stand back and take it all in. Our renovated house is quite spectacular, created and supported by many parts—the quality and value of the entire structure increase when each section is up to standard. However, the whole thing would collapse in the wind without a solid foundation, sturdy inner structure, and impenetrable roof. It's the same for our inner being. If it's out of balance, the slightest trigger can send us tumbling down in an avalanche of emotions.

Throughout this book, we compare the interior workings of a house with our chakras. When there's an issue on an upper level of our house, we must figure out where the problem originated below. And within our bodies, our entire system is affected when our chakras are blocked. The energy centers running The House of You seem imperceptible. Yet, their power, whether weak or full throttle, affects every aspect of our being.

While these seven main chakras work as independent energy regulators within us, they are integral to each other. When we're working on one aspect, the other parts are involved. Therefore, the chakras and the body, mind, and spirit create an indivisible whole, intrinsic to our being. Our chakras hold our life stories and inform us of our strengths and weaknesses. And it's imperative to consider the whole when seeking self-empowerment and manifestation.

Let's unfold the architect's blueprint and get a bird's-eye view of the whole House of You. Consider that the chakras are often depicted in an outline of the body sitting cross-legged in the lotus position. The chakras line up with the spine from the tailbone to the crown.

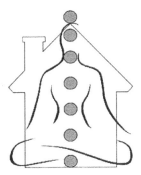

In this image of The House of You with the chakras, notice how the physical body aligns with the virtual renovation house drawing. The 1st Chakra, the Root, overlays the foundation. The 2nd Chakra, the Sacral, is in the basement. Continuing through the house are the following four chakras: Solar Plexus, Heart, Throat, and Third Eye. And at the top sits the Crown Chakra.

Imagine enhancing the picture with the chakra colors. Sketching this double image in your journal can help you remember the chakras' positions in your body.

Knowing the chakras' locations helps you heal as you practice noticing and feeling bodily sensations more often. When the feelings in your body point out which chakras are blocked, tap for the physical and emotional indicators coming from the shadow wanting your attention.

Use this blueprint and your chakra system to identify and release any blocks. Then, when stressed, we can tap and scan our bodies for any physical feelings and sensations. Remember, when thoughts are whirling in our minds, we're not in our bodies. We're not present. And we need to be in alignment. Fortunately, we've learned that breathing and tapping bring us out of our heads and into our bodies. As we calm our nerves, our thinking clears. This shift happens in an instant.

The inspection process is the same as searching our house for the source of a problem. No hot water in an upstairs bathroom is a sign. It might be a busted water heater in the basement. Likewise, pain or sensations in our bodies correlate with nearby chakras. For instance, a rumbly tummy indicates the 2nd Chakra, which sits below our navel. Tapping on the physical issue first makes us curious about the emotions beneath it—profound stress reduction and healing occur.

Refer to my example in Chapter Five of *Your Playbook* of Tapping in the Shower for lower back pain. Fear came through when I tapped and voiced the acute pain. I didn't know why I might be afraid. I only knew the shadow called "fear" wanted my attention. Once I tapped and acknowledged fear's presence, the stuck energy moved. And the back pain dissipated.

Discomforts or odd feelings can emerge in more than one area of your body. Work on the most prominent sensation or pain first. The intensity in one spot causes constriction elsewhere. An initial release of the primary energy often lessens the other physical and emotional issues.

Take, for example, a queasy stomach, which sits in your 3rd Chakra, the seat of action. Feeling into your body, you may notice your chest is tight and your heart is pounding. Then, after only a few minutes of tapping, your stomach calms, your heart rate lowers, and the tightness in your chest subsides. Finally, your brain stops fighting, and an aha moment hits.

These typical sensations show up when there's strong resistance in the 4th Chakra. It pushes back on your attempts to step up into action. Then the struggle manifests as indigestion, nausea, heartburn, or worse. And the Heart Chakra's shadows don't feel safe to take action.

Feelings can surface as nervous butterflies or paralyzing fear. These reactions are protective mechanisms created by our shadows in fear for our safety. Becoming aware of feelings and emotions reminds us to stop, breathe, and tap. With tapping, our nerves settle, and thinking clears. Once we're grounded, our emotions arise. Looking inward, we can see how past experiences contribute to our present thoughts. Then we can address the root causes of those thoughts and feelings.

Identify areas of unease in the body to pinpoint chakras and shadows needing attention. When you decipher which chakra may connect with that part of your body, revisit that chakra's chapter in this book to review the relevant stories and insights to help you move the trapped energy.

Check out your Chapter Eleven Chakra Balancing homeplay.

In the middle of my transformational journey,
I discovered the girl I put aside at twenty.
Finding that forgotten part reminds me of Dorothy in
The Wizard of Oz. Our power is ever present; we've always had it.
We empower ourselves by learning to excavate doubt
and returning home to The House of You.
—Sandy Evenson, *The Woo Woo Way*

Thank You for Visiting,
A Letter from The House of You

Dear Self,

I am your inner house. You were open-minded and brave and completed your first walkthrough. Now there's a new understanding, a new way of seeing. While discovering my inner beauty, you found your own. You have everything you need here inside The House of You.

Thank you for allowing yourself to be vulnerable and shining a light on my dark side. Your shadows hiding here are grateful for your acknowledgment. And your continued attention ensures all seven energy centers can function with precision.

I'm a complete stand-alone structure and the sum of all parts of you. Every aspect does its designated job and contributes to running the entire house.

Your thorough inspection brought some exciting discoveries. The forgotten shadow characteristics came forward after you rejected and pushed them down. They showed you spectacular hidden gems you didn't know you possessed. And your investigative chakra work sparked an emotional evolution, bringing the shadow into the light.

Please take a moment to observe me and be open to loving every part of you.

Your assignment, should you choose to accept it, is to love and maintain every part of you. The House of You ownership includes accepting your lower self, the source of your empowerment energy. For your light side to access Source Energy, you must acknowledge your dark side, which requires the same attention and recognition as your Higher Self. The key to reaching enlightenment is clearing your chakras. When unblocked, your higher and lower self energies join in your Heart Chakra.

All systems flow within you when you align with the vibration of your higher power; then manifestation follows.

Be proud of your first walkthrough. Create a to-do list and keep returning to your inner home. Uncover, clear, and heal the blocks in your chakras.

Layer by precious layer, discover the unmined jewels embedded within you. Be curious. Be forgiving. Give yourself compassion for what you endured, your wounds, and the love you lost.

Your self-knowledge empowers you, and your house is solid. Now you have the maintenance tools to strengthen and support every aspect of you.

Welcome home.

Thank You for Visiting, A Letter from The House of You
https://youtu.be/k34-ijnwxDs

SCAN ME

Acknowledgments

> We need to understand that there is no formula
> for how women should lead their lives.
> That is why we must respect the choices that
> each woman makes for herself and her family.
> Every woman deserves the chance to realize
> her God-given potential.
> —Hillary Rodham Clinton, *It Takes a Village*

As I express my gratitude, I remember the proverb, "It takes a village to raise a child." It conveys the message that it takes many people to provide a safe, healthy environment for children to grow, flourish, and realize their hopes and dreams. A book or other object of creativity can feel like our "baby." I, too, needed a village of writing, editing, publishing, and marketing specialists shepherding *The Woo Woo Way* from its inception through development and launch.

Initially, I set out to write a small freebie to help build my email list. And then it grew into the book in your hands (or on the screen). During my fifteen-month book-writing journey, I met many creative people who joined my village and supported me. I watched in awe as my manuscript was handled with care, nurtured, and passed from one expert to another. With humble adoration, I thank the many people who contributed to the inspiration and creation of this book.

First, I thank Cindy Childress, PhD, who reawakened my love of storytelling during her "Success Stories" course in the spring of 2021. Then in September, I enrolled in her premiere course, "Crank Out Your Book in Eight Weeks." Dr. Cindy, The Expert's Ghostwriter, book-writing coach, and mentor, helped develop my writing style.

She even saw my signature seven major chakra framework before I did. Finally, I had my messy first draft and took the course a second time to perfect it. Upon completion, I hired her for the developmental editing. She waved her fairy book-mother wand over my manuscript, and all the pieces fell into place. Cindy's enthusiastic encouragement, praise, support, and endless resources kept me on track to get over the finish line and be a published author.

Thanks also to Cindy for introducing me to Everett O'Keefe of Ignite Press, who referred me to Becky Norwood of Spotlight Publishing House. I felt an instant connection with Becky and knew I was in the right place. She offered everything I needed and more I hadn't thought of yet. She has created a beautiful step-by-step process for her authors to succeed—in-depth book launch knowledge, publishing expertise, and marketing materials. Becky's passion inspires me in how she supports her authors to become #1 Bestsellers—she has the tools and personnel to get us there.

Once we completed the developmental editing, I needed to find a copy editor. Who knew there was more than one kind of editing? After Becky introduced me to several copy editors to interview, I chose Lynn Thompson of Living on Purpose Communications. I thank Lynn for creating a collaborative approach in editing my book, chapter by chapter, line by line. With some of my lessons, she helped assemble bridges to connect ideas. Editing takes focused time, so it's great that we often laughed with abandon and talked aloud to Grammarly. There's nothing better than a good belly laugh for healing. How perfect, since healing is the theme of my book.

Thanks to Maggie Mongan of Brilliant Breakthroughs, Inc., author and master business coach, and Marketing Visibility Partner at Spotlight Publishing House. Maggie is well-versed in all things woo with extensive background and training. Skilled at creating essential marketing assets, Maggie has been invaluable for effectively expressing my brand, expertise, and passion for my audience.

Thanks to Arden Reece, of Arden Reece Color, for her guidance. She's gifted with psychic sight and is an expert in the messages color speaks about us. She taught me how to use color to increase my confidence, well-being, and even my level of enlightenment. Arden updated my logo and branding, tweaking the colors to express my essence and create a consistent message. When I saw what she produced, I said, "Oh, wow, this is me!"

I'm grateful for Patsy Balacchi of Zenotica, my front cover designer. She understood what I was trying to convey and created a masterpiece. The brilliant colors of the seven major chakras flow up the book's front cover with ethereal grace and beauty.

Thanks to Blair Hornbuckle, my photographer friend, for helping me shine as my authentic self through his brilliant, creative portraiture.

I am grateful for the email from Hay House promoting Nick Ortner's book *The Tapping Solution*. Thanks to Nick for his passion, commitment, and drive to bring EFT tapping to the world. Thanks also to Nick's sister Jessica Ortner for her soft, melodic, and hypnotic voice on the tapping audios. When I felt my world crashing down, Jessica and Nick were the angels I needed to jolt me out of my overwhelming anxiety.

Thanks again to Nick for introducing me to Margaret Lynch Raniere, my coach trainer and mentor. While tapping eased my stress, Margaret's deep inner work led to profound revelations about myself. I learned to see with my inner vision and trust what my unconscious mind wanted to show me. As a result, the girl I put aside at twenty awakened with a renewed zest for life, and I found a new purpose in becoming a coach with Margaret's guidance.

I appreciate the four women in The Core Coach Mastermind who supported and encouraged me to follow through on writing this book. Thanks to Donna McGurk, Irene Jorgensen, Ina Bachman, and Kay Walker.

I am thankful for the people who raised and shaped me. My parents gave me love and instilled a sense of dignity, curiosity, awe, and wonder. My dad showed me how to use an encyclopedia, observe the moon and stars, and tickled my funny bone. Mom fueled an awareness of beauty everywhere we went. Special thanks to my grandparents, aunts, and uncles—the satellite of support for my siblings and me. They gave me a strong sense of self-worth, ensuring this shy, fragile girl could thrive in the world.

Special thanks to the close friends who supported me during my husband Dennis' long decline in health. Doug Evenson, my late husband's youngest brother, and his wife, Julie, loved Dennis as much as I did and helped me navigate the rough spots. I express my beyond-words gratitude to Maria Lancaster for everything, including checking in on me each day. Thanks to my chef friend, Roxanne Koteles, for your Green Smooth Juice that sustained me through those long chaotic hours with Dennis in the hospital and assisted living. I appreciate her coming to help and stay with me during the hurricane. I also thank Roxanne for inviting me to attend a retreat with her at Hilton Head, South Carolina. The timing was perfect for me as a needed break from Dennis' intense and worsening mental state.

I appreciate the hair salon clients who opened themselves up to me, helping me build a valuable skill—empathic listening.

Immense gratitude goes to my coaching clients for trusting me on their transformational journey. By sharing their stories of self-discovery and healing, they graciously said "Yes" to helping others. I'm honored to continue my mission to evoke beauty from the inside out for the women I'm privileged to meet.

Thank you, Universe, for showing me the opportunities for two incredible careers—hairdressing and coaching. And I'm blessed twice with two great loves—my late husband and Ray Justice. Ray stepped into my life at Julie Colvin's Wellness & Writing Retreat as a writer friend. During weekly phone chats, Ray and I discussed doing a joint writing project on beauty. Each call began with Ray prompting me to vent my intense frustrations. Then, after listening to my exuberant rant, he found laughter in me. Those calls always left me feeling lighter and free as we developed our friendship. His strong presence and kind heart buoyed my resilience to face another week of caregiving. I built a wall around my heart to keep him from getting too close, but he saw through me. Many thanks to Ray for waiting for me and giving me the space, time, and patience to transition from caregiver to life partner. He encouraged and supported me every step of the way into his arms. I'm grateful that I could incorporate some of Ray's stress-reducing techniques into my homeplay exercises in *Your Playbook.*

During the final days of Dennis' decline, I used tapping to keep my frustration and anxiety at bay. With alcoholic dementia, he was like a four-year-old, unable to understand what I wanted to convey. On the day that they rushed him by ambulance to the hospital, I was on my way from the airport, crying and tapping on the steering wheel. I begged God to let him go, telling Dennis energetically that I would be okay and he could let go. When I arrived at the emergency room, the doctor said that Dennis had died in the ambulance with no pain. When I saw his body, he had a slight smile, and all his physical symptoms had vanished—wrinkles, swollenness, redness—I knew his spirit was finally at peace.

Thank you to Carolyn Milton, CEO of Handle with Loving Care LLC, and her team for their specialized caregiving and genuine love for Dennis.

Thank you to Debra Anthony Larson and the entire Hospice Savannah staff. Since I was still working full-time in the salon, I was grateful to express my gratitude by caring for your hair as you cared for Dennis.

My transformational journey birthed my desire to share the profound impact of these techniques and processes for your benefit—sincere thanks to everyone reading or listening to this book. My heart is full.

About the Author

A shy Catholic schoolgirl, Sandy Evenson went from high school to microbiology lab tech in the Army and from there to cosmetology school. Combining her love of art and science through over four decades, she enjoyed a stellar career as an award-winning hairdresser/colorist for men, women, and children. While enhancing each client's external image, she observed countless transformations for women in self-confidence and self-worth. Sandy loved illuminating their inner beauty. Embracing her motto, Beauty from the Inside Out, she helped each woman look good and *feel* great. Her passion and empathy grew through connecting with women who felt safe to let their hair down and bare their souls.

While Sandy could have continued working in the salon, she yearned for more independence and time to write, travel, volunteer, and contribute in a meaningful way. Working with people within the sanctity of the styling chair prepared Sandy for a new career in women's empowerment coaching. After overlapping her work in the salon with innumerable transformative hours of intensive coach training, Sandy retired from the beauty industry, a career she loved and cherished.

As an award-winning master coach, Sandy shines a light on the hidden emotional blocks that hold women back, taking them on a life-changing journey to reclaim their inner power. Sandy shares a wealth of knowledge and expertise with her intuitive coaching processes centered around visualization, active imagination, chakra clearing, and shadow work. She customizes each program for individuals and groups by incorporating the Emotional Freedom Technique, EFT tapping into her sessions.

Sandy leads her coaching programs with heart, compassion, and non-judgmental curiosity. She shares powerful, stress-reducing techniques to relieve unnecessary physical and emotional suffering. Held in a cocoon of safety, women can let go of fear, anxiety, frustration, sadness, and loss and attain optimal health, weight, prosperity, loving relationships, and peace. And as they release negative emotions, an inner life-force energy ignites empowered confidence, passion, enthusiasm, and joy.

While working as a hairdresser, Sandy compared transformations that occur with hair color and style makeovers to caterpillars changing into the wondrous beauty of butterflies. Now, Sandy witnesses true inner metamorphosis while showing wise, ageless women how to uncover their hidden blocks to success, realize their dreams and shine their best lives. Women around the world praise Sandy's insightful coaching methods. Sandy's passionate drive to teach women self-empowerment inspired her to write *The Woo Woo Way, Unblock Your Chakras and Transform Your Life*.

Sandy resides in Rochester, New York, with her life partner, Ray Justice, and Milo the cat, aka Dude. When not writing, she enjoys pre-dawn and evening meditation with oracle cards, working out with weights, power walking in nature, strolling through city streets, and being creative with art, cooking, photography, interior decorating, and writing.

YOUR WOO WOO WAY PLAYBOOK

Chakra Homeplay

SANDY EVENSON

Our ultimate power comes from
working on ourselves,
because when we work on ourselves,
everyone else changes.
—Christian Mickelsen, *Abundance Unleashed*

Your Playbook Contents

Introduction

While we are a lot less familiar with addressing life
at this body-sensation/energy level
of our being, doing so is actually the easiest,
quickest route to healing and wholeness.
—Dr. Sue Morter, *The Energy Codes*

Your Woo Woo Playbook Introduction
https://youtu.be/lATh-Yz6iRI

SCAN ME

Welcome to *Your Woo Woo Way Playbook*. It was so tough to choose what homeplay to give you that I included additional exercises at the end of *Your Playbook*. I've given you everything I can think of to get started transforming your life.

I recorded *Your Playbook* for you and I encourage you to tap along with me. Relax and close your eyes during the visualizations and guided meditations.

Allow me to guide you through the homeplay. After you've experienced the exercises, revisit them as needed. You may discover that an underlying emotion appears as you clear a block. Keep tapping to continue making progress. The homeplay helps you get the most out of your inner work.

Use tapping to quiet your inner critic as you explore your thoughts, ideas, and memories on paper. Your journaling is just for your reading and reflection. Decide later if you want to share and with whom.

Use *Your Playbook* your way. First, follow along with each chapter's homeplay to get a feel for the exercises. Then, put your spin on them, in your words—for any given circumstance, feeling, and emotion.

Ignite your inner power, tap into your brilliance, and shine your best life with *The Woo Woo Way.*

Shine Brightly,
Sandy Evenson

YOUR HOMEPLAY

Chapter One

TAP INTO HEALING

*Each time I Tap, I am continually amazed at the way it helps me to calm down, find peace, and relax into trusting that **all is well**.*
—Nick Ortner, *The Tapping Solution*

I'm passionate about EFT tapping because of its profound effect on me. It helped me through one of the most challenging times of my life and saved my sanity. Tapping calmed my emotional reactions to people and situations. After experiencing the rapid reduction of stress, I continued to tap whenever I felt triggered. As a result, my inner fear, anxiety, and self-doubt, shifted into groundedness and sound decision-making. That shift lifted me from surviving, wondering what to do in the next phase of my life, to thriving with purpose and clarity. My profound tapping experience inspired me to become a coach and help others regain control and shine their best lives. Thus, *The Woo Woo Way* was born!

As I demonstrate through my story, incorporate tapping as a potent mind-body tool to relieve stress, alleviate pain, and revitalize energy. The tapping exercises here in *Your Playbook* assume that you have a base level of knowledge about EFT, and the chapters walk you through the seven major chakras of your internal energy system.

First, we learn basic tapping to reduce stress and physical pain. Then, to achieve our true desires, deeper introspection is required, and tapping helps us feel safe while uncovering our hidden truths.

Practice using the Emotional Freedom Technique (EFT) tapping.

What is EFT Tapping?
https://youtu.be/E_3npLJiUjg

How to Tap
https://youtu.be/YbwIRdcJOv8

SCAN ME

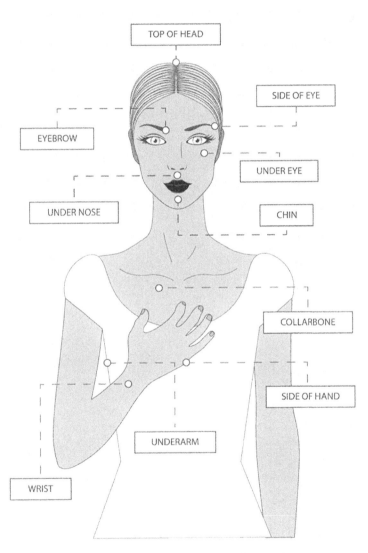

Customized graphic design by Arden Reece for sandyevenson.com

Chapter Two

TAPPING FOR STRESS

The primary cause of unhappiness is never the situation
but your thoughts about it.
—Eckhart Tolle, *Oneness With All Life*

https://youtu.be/x2XjYz58dbk

SCAN ME

Have you heard of the 5-4-3-2-1 Method for stress reduction and grounding? It's a simple process that often has a calming effect. By concentrating on the things in your environment, you draw your focus away from any anxious thoughts. Combining the 5-4-3-2-1 Method with tapping results in a more powerful grounding, helping you move out of your head and into your body. Your heart rate slows, and your breathing eases. Relaxing into a calmer state, you gain a new perspective on handling stressful situations. The process only takes 30 to 60 seconds, and you can do it sitting down or walking around.

The 5-4-3-2-1 Method with
Tapping for maximum calming

Use this process when your mind is full of anxious, worrisome thoughts.

1. Start tapping. You may choose to tap through all the tapping points or on one point only.

2. Engage your five senses, noticing what's in the world around you.
*   ***See 5 things***
    It could be a pencil, a spot on the wall, or notice anything in your surroundings.
*   ***Touch 4 items***
    It might be your face, clothing, chair, or rug.
*   ***Hear 3 sounds***
    Notice external sounds beyond your body, noise from traffic and birds outside, the refrigerator, or a fan.
*   ***Smell 2 aromas***
    Maybe it's the scent of coffee, flowers, hand soap, or lotion.
*   ***Taste 1 thing***
    A mint on your tongue, sip water, or taste the air.

3. Linger in the moment, relaxed, and renewed.

4. Engage your sense of humor, intuition, and curiosity.

5. Record your impressions in your journal, if you wish.

Chapter Three

AFFIRMATION ENERGY TAPPING

Feelings are the antennae of the soul.
—Anodea Judith, *Eastern Body, Western Mind*

https://youtu.be/uK2SjkaVgRI

SCAN ME

Did Missy's story in Chapter Three of *The Woo Woo Way* resonate with you? Are you wondering when it's going to be your time to shine? Do you need help making affirmations to achieve your desired outcomes?

1. Start by writing a list. Make it a big one. Be specific and write down all the things and experiences you can imagine, from a new car to a walk on the beach with someone you love who loves you. When it comes to fulfilling your dreams, the options are limitless.

2. If you wish, you can create a vision board with images representing your envisioned future.

3. Next, visualize all aspects of your dream being real. What are your feelings? Often, they're simple yet profound—joy, peace, fulfillment, acknowledgment, and freedom.

4. Now practice getting into that feeling. Place your list where you can see it every day. Tap as you read your list.

5. From your emotions, create affirmations in the present tense, beginning with "I am." You can use phrases such as: "I am happy." "I am ecstatic." "I am at peace." I am healthy, fit, and fabulous." "I am prosperous."

6. Tap while reciting each affirmation.

Affirmations are an integral part of the Law of Attraction. Expressing joy amplifies your joy.

1. The last step is letting go of the outcome. Focus on the feelings. When you fixate on exact things, you may miss something bigger that The Universe has in store.

2. Every day, read your list or look at your vision board, tap, repeat your affirmations, and say, "This or something better." You are co-creating with Spirit. Let go and let God.

Affirmations work when you embody the feelings inspired by your burning desires. Working through the chakras in the following chapters helps you acknowledge and clear self-doubt.

Start with these affirmations:

"I am open to looking deep within to reclaim my manifestation power."
"I am open to releasing resistance to change."
"I am open to attracting joy, love, and peace."

Chapter Four

1ˢᵀ CHAKRA
TAPPING FOR ANXIETY

While they cannot be seen or held as material entities,
the chakras are evident in the shape of our physical bodies,
the patterns manifested in our lives, and the way we think,
feel, and handle situations that life presents us. Just as we see
the wind through movement of the leaves and branches,
the chakras can be seen by what we create around us.
—Anodea Judith, *Eastern Body, Western Mind*

https://youtu.be/XTFzO1eQPGE

SCAN ME

1ˢᵗ Chakra
Name: Root, *Affirmation:* I Am, *My Right:* To Be Here
Themes: Empowered Stability, Energy, Comfort, Safety, Security
Primary Issues: Safety, Security, and Survival
Location in the Body: Base of the Spine
In The House of You: The Foundation
Color Resonance: Red, *Chakra Wisdom Crystal:* Ruby
Developmental Stage: Womb to 18 Months

Tapping for Anxiety

This technique is my go-to tapping process to address anxiety. When you feel intense stress or overwhelm, jump right in and tap. You can choose to tap on all the tapping points or just one. Sometimes it helps to stand or walk around while tapping. You can tap anywhere at any time.

Buffer down the intensity of your anxiety.

1. Think about a recent event or situation where you felt stressed.

2. Start tapping and say out loud, or to yourself, everything that's on your mind. Express all the negative emotions that arise, such as frustration, anger, and sadness.

3. Notice and voice any discomfort, pain, or unease in your body.

4. Turn your thoughts into words and phrases as you rotate through the tapping points.

5. Move to the next point each time you express an emotion, or continue to tap one point. I tend to tap on the collarbone point.

6. *You can't do this wrong.* Tap and voice your emotions, feelings, and sensations until you feel a shift in your body as the magnitude of your issue decreases.

Use this sample script and add or substitute your own words, vocalizing whatever is on your mind.

Tapping Script

Oh my God, I'm so stressed.
All this anxiety.
Too much stress.
I'm really worried.
There is so much going on.
I don't know what to do.
I can't cope with this.
I'm really scared.
I'm so frightened.
I can't think straight.
What am I going to do?
I'm so angry.
Frustrated.
I hate this.
It isn't fair.
Why did he say that?
I shouldn't have said anything.
What's going to happen now?
I'm so upset.
I can't deal with this.
What if?
I'm terrified.
I can't believe this is happening.
My heart is pounding.
My neck is killing me.
My stomach is churning.
All this anxiety.
I can hardly breathe.
Too much stress.
Anxiety and fear are taking me down.
I'm so frustrated.

This is maddening.
God, I'm so stressed.
I'm so anxious.
All this anxiety.
This is maddening.

Note: It isn't necessary to fix it right now or add positive affirmations. Just voice it, honor it, and clear it.

Tapping Script

I'm just going to honor how I feel.
I honor how much stress I'm under.
And how much pain I have.
I honor how anxious I feel.
I honor my fear.
I'm just gonna honor how I feel.
I honor how much I've been thorough.
And how much I'm going through.

This type of tapping is fast and effective. It only takes a minute or two to leave suffering and worry behind. I have tapped several times a day during overwhelming stress. For example, I rinsed dishes in the kitchen sink with one hand while tapping on my collarbone point with the other. In thirty seconds, I lowered my anxiety and frustration. Throughout your day, even if you don't think you're anxious, pause, gently push the soles of your feet against the floor, and notice your breath. You may clear anxious thoughts before they intensify.

Feeling calmer now? These simple mindful moments bring you out of your busy mind, ground you, and buffer stress.

Chapter Five

2ND CHAKRA
TALKING TO YOUR SHADOW

Reclaiming the parts of ourselves that we have relegated to the shadow is the most reliable path to actualizing all of our human potential.
—Debbie Ford, *The Shadow Effect*

https://youtu.be/UQ-5HYl3MuY

SCAN ME

2nd Chakra
Name: Sacral, *Affirmation:* I Feel, *My Right:* To Feel and To Have
Themes: Empowered Creativity, Passion, Desires, Needs, Sensuality, Sexuality, and Sociability
Primary Issues: Sensuality, Sexuality, Emotions, and Creativity
Location in the Body: Abdomen, Just Below the Navel
In The House of You: The Basement
Color Resonance: Orange
Chakra Wisdom Crystal: Orange Carnelian
Developmental Stage: Six Months to Two Years

Talking to Your Shadow 1.0

In this exercise, use your imagination. Let your shadow speak and tell you why it holds you back. Your simple acknowledgment quiets the shadow in minutes.

1. Find a quiet place where you can remain undisturbed. Give yourself as much time as you need.

2. After you read my story, use my tapping script for your conversation with your shadow.

3. Insert or substitute your own words for the emotions and feelings.

4. Listen to what this part of you has to say. Then, give it a new job and ask it to work with you.

Notice what comes up. It's gold.

My example of talking to my shadow

I woke up one day with a nagging ache in my lower back. It grew into intense pain. I realized the issue wasn't muscular or skeletal. My lower back flares up from time to time. Too much sugar, caffeine, or wine often affects my kidneys. The usual remedies didn't work. The pain was relentless. I'd learned how the organs in our bodies hold emotions. For example, our kidneys store fear, so my back pain signaled that fear wanted my attention. I needed to acknowledge this fear underlying the physical pain.

There's an energetic benefit to tapping in the shower or tub. The negative feelings and emotions wash down the drain. There's something to that Rogers and Hammerstein's song from *South Pacific*, "I'm gonna wash that man right outta my hair."

The following script contains the gist of my tapping conversation with fear.

Tapping Script

Hello FEAR.
Why are you here?
Why am I afraid?
I can't figure it out.
What's going on?
I know that you want to protect me.
I know that you love me.
And I know that you would be devastated
to know that you are hurting me.
I appreciate you.
You have been with me my whole life.
At times when I needed it most.
You're using an old method, though.
An old reptilian method.
It does not work anymore.
You're hurting me.
You've been holding me back.
And holding me down.
I know you've got my back.
Oh my God, you've literally got my back.
It's okay.
You can let go now.
You can loosen your grip.
I am grateful for everything you've done for me.
This old method isn't working anymore.
We need a new way.
My way.
You can relax your hold and stand down.
Stand at ease.
You can come with me.
I know you're not going anywhere.

You can be my bodyguard.
Or my lookout.
Or my guardian angel.
You can stand beside me.
In front of me.
Or behind me.
Just let go of your tight grip on me.
Maybe you could whisper in my ear.
Or tap me on the shoulder.
I promise to listen.
I won't ignore you.
You can point out the red flags I need to see.
I can stop and look around, take a breath, and ask:
What do I need to see?
What do I need to know?
To hear?
To feel?
To smell?
Or taste?
Thank you for being here.
I am open to letting go of being afraid.
And I am open to the possibilities ahead for me.

I stepped out of the shower. *Oh wow, there's no pain.* You read that right; the pain was gone. I was stunned at how it worked for me. I don't know why it surprised me that this short tapping process was so effective since I often see similar results with my clients. Of course, I can't guarantee such fast relief for everyone. However, tapping while talking to your shadow relaxes your body.

I didn't know what I was afraid of that day. Giving the shadow space to be acknowledged was all it needed to clear from my system. The tapping diminished my frustration and anxiety caused by physical and emotional pain.

Talking to Your Shadow 2.0

From my shower story, you learned it's possible to go deeper by talking to your shadow. Now do your tapping process on the feeling or emotion you're experiencing:

1. Listen for the negative words in your head. How do you feel when you hear that voice?

2. Notice where in your body you feel physical sensations of unease, discomfort, tightness, or pain.

3. What emotion is in this sensation? If you don't know, guess. Your subconscious mind tells you what you need to hear.

4. Check in with how you feel physically and emotionally.

5. Follow my fear-tapping script from my story and insert your specific emotion and pain. Or tap on whatever's on your mind.

6. You may cry, yawn, cough, sneeze, burp, or fart while tapping. It's all energy, and it's moving.

7. Keep tapping until you feel a shift in your body—lighter with less negative emotion.

8. You don't have to fix anything. Acknowledge it, voice it, honor it. I often say, "I'm just going to honor how I feel."

Revisit this homeplay whenever an emotion or physical symptom has a grip on you.

Chapter Six

3RD CHAKRA
STEPPING INTO ACTION

I am not what happened to me. I am what I choose to become.
—Carl Jung

https://youtu.be/tqrikyHNyOI

SCAN ME

3rd Chakra
Name: Solar Plexus
Affirmation: I Do
My Right: To Act
Themes: Empowered Strength, Personality, Power, and Determination
Primary Issues: Power, Strength of Will, and Purpose
Location in the Body: Upper Abdomen, Just Below Ribcage
In The House of You: The Great Room
Color Resonance: Yellow
Chakra Wisdom Crystal: Citrine
Developmental Stage: Eighteen Months to Four Years

Stepping Into Action

This tapping process differs from the others in *Your Playbook*. Unblocking procrastination involves tapping and ranting at ourselves. While tapping, we curse, swear, and call ourselves ignorant, inept losers for procrastinating.

Once again, we are moving the energy, clearing the 3rd Chakra. We harvest its power to act and create the lives we desire.

Note: I adapted portions of this exercise from Colette Baron-Reid's Invision Process ®.

Here are your Stepping into Action homeplay instructions:

1.   Find a comfortable place to sit where you won't be disturbed.

2.   Bring whatever is bothering you to mind. Let the scene play out.

3.   As you contemplate these questions, tap through the points or on just one point, such as the collarbone.

4.   What emotion am I feeling?

5.   Where do I feel it in my body?

6.   See or feel yourself in this picture with your inner vision.

7.   Then ask, "Where am I?"

8.   Once you know where you are, ask, "When am I?"

9.   The answer to where and when is often the same. Are you dwelling on a problem from the past? Or are you worried about what happens next, in the future?

10. Either way, it means that you are not present.

11. Notice your mind chatter.

12. Now ask, "Who am I listening to?"

13. Continue to tap. Let your body and subconscious mind help you identify your inner saboteur. Most of the time, you can recognize the voice. It could be your mother, father, sibling, uncle, fifth-grade teacher, ex, or shadow.

14. Sometimes, there's a whole committee in your head, a gang of misfits causing trouble.

15. Take a breath when you recognize the sabotaging voice that stops your attempts to move forward. And declare it out loud.

    "I am not this critical voice. It isn't me. I feel sad. But I am not a sad person. I have a needy side. *And* I am strong. There's a part of me that's angry. But I'm not an angry woman."

16. Disengage from your self-critical voices.

17. Be curious. Make statements such as, "Isn't that interesting?" or "That's interesting. I wonder what it means," or "What created this feeling in me?"

18. Move out of the challenging dialogue. Instead, become a neutral observer and ask yourself one more question: "What meaning am I giving to this issue?"

19. Is the story you tell yourself *the* truth? Or is it *your* truth? Rather than bypass the issue, address it and respond instead of react.

20. Take a breath, observe a different perspective, and awaken a new appreciation for the experience.

None of us would be where we are today if it weren't for everything we've been through, all the good and the bad. When we take the time to tap, we voice all the wrongdoings and unfair treatment that occurred. Then, our adult understanding brings compassion for ourselves and the others involved. The facts as you remember them have not changed. However, you are no longer the victim of the story.

Change your story, transform your life.
—Colette Baron-Reid

4TH CHAKRA
HEALING YOUR HEART

You see, I was still making decisions based
on the experiences and scars
of an eight-year-old, and those deep cuts
and broken bonds of security
that I had not yet actively learned to replace.
—Sharon Stone, *The Beauty of Living Twice*

https://youtu.be/OT4ef3dUwDg

SCAN ME

4th Chakra
Name: Heart, *Affirmation:* I Love, *My Right:* To Love
Themes: Empowered Acceptance, Love, Compassion, and Sincerity
Primary Issues: Love and Relationships
Location in the Body: Chest Area
In The House of You: The Kitchen
Color Resonance: Green
Chakra Wisdom Crystal: Emerald
Developmental Stage: Four to Seven Years

Healing Your Heart

This heart-healing homeplay assists in unblocking your Heart Chakra. Practicing this technique at the end of your day is incredibly beneficial because when your heart clears, you can let go of pent-up stress and negative emotions. Then, a restful good night's sleep ensues.

This exercise blends tapping with techniques from Ray Justice, HeartMath, and David R. Hamilton, PhD.

Follow these steps for Healing Your Heart:

1. Find a comfortable place to sit or lie down without being disturbed or distracted. Uncross your arms and legs.

2. Notice the thoughts cycling through your mind. Rate your stress or heartache from the lowest zero to the highest of ten. Sense where you feel tightness and constriction in your body.

3. Picture your troublesome thoughts and prevalent issues. Then use your hands to physically push the problem away from you in a sweeping motion.

4. Start tapping through the points while taking slow, easy breaths. Feel your lungs filling with air. Breathe deeper, noticing your belly rise and fall with your breath. Now bring your attention to your heart. Imagine your breath flowing in and out as if your heart is breathing for you.

5. Breathe and tap, soft and slow, as you contemplate acts of kindness.

Use one or all of the following examples:

- Recall kindness demonstrated by someone you know. Think about what you admire about that person.
- Remember witnessing an act of kindness by a stranger.

- Reflect on acts of kindness you did for other people. Or examine the way someone supported you.

6. Stop tapping. Continue your slow, deep, refreshing breaths and sense the feeling of experiencing kindness.

7. Hover your hand above your chest and focus on your heart. Breathe deeply, concentrating on your breath flowing in and out of your heart.

8. Trace your fingertips across your chest and bring in a sense of appreciation. Feel the energy vibrating from your heart. Stay in the appreciation vibe for a few more breaths.

9. Open your arms, imagine someone you care about, and send your love and appreciation to them.

10. See the other person in your mind's eye. Then, imagine breathing this energy of love in a circle from your heart to theirs and back to yours. Repeat three times or more.

11. Cross your hands over your heart. Feel love and appreciation.

12. Tap with the fingers of the hand closest to your body. Follow the script. Feel free to add or substitute your own words.

Tapping Script

I feel warmth in my heart.
And I am open to filling my heart with love.
I've had a lot of heartache.
I've endured a lot of pain.
I am open to letting go of past wounds.
And allowing some love in.
One small step at a time.
I know I have a lot of work to do here.

I'm not quite done with these wounds.
Manifesting my desired future.
Depends on the healing I've done.
And the forgiveness work I'm doing.
I am open to lowering my shield.
I am open to letting love in.
And sharing my heart with others.
Now that I'm aware of my wounds.
I can heal them.
I honor how I feel.
My heart has been broken.
Many times.
But I am not broken.
I am breaking through.
And I give myself the space to heal.
Because I am on the right path.
For my highest good.
And greatest joy.
And the highest good of all.

13. If you're lying down, you may drift off into a peaceful sleep.

Otherwise, take a deep breath, move your arms and shake your hands to release excess energy. You can move your feet and shake your whole body if you wish. Shake it out.

14. Re-assess your stress level, 0 – 10. If your number has increased, you've hit on something that needs more attention. Keep going. Repeat the tapping and include any new emotions that come up.

Throughout the day, spinning thoughts may often recur in your mind. When you notice it happening, take a breath and return to the present moment. Start tapping. It is like pushing "reset" when your home alarm system accidentally goes off. You're letting go of old stories and wounds. Fill your open heart with love and appreciation. And know that you are loved.

Chapter Eight

5ᵀᴴ CHAKRA PHONE HOME

A Crowded Mind . . . Can Not Listen.
—Ray Justice, *Ideas to Wonder*

https://youtu.be/TVS4rjIoI_E

SCAN ME

5ᵗʰ Chakra
Name: Throat
Affirmation: I Speak
My Right: To Speak
Themes: Empowered Communication, Expression, Inspiration, Resonance, and Voice
Primary Issues: Communication and Engagement
Location in the Body: Neck Area
In The House of You: The Mezzanine
Color Resonance: Blue
Chakra Wisdom Crystal: Sapphire
Developmental Stage: Seven to Twelve Years

Phone Home

Clear your Throat Chakra by expressing yourself with breath, movement, and sound. Then we invite your authentic voice to Phone Home. It's kind of like the movie *E.T. the Extra-Terrestrial*. This voice is often lost and estranged. It's time to reconnect.

Note: I have adapted this homeplay from *Eastern Body, Western Mind* by Anodea Judith.

Follow this process for Phone Home:

1. Find a comfortable space where you can make noise and have room to move your body.

2. While standing, stretch upward, reaching for the sky. Stretch to the right and left, forward and back, loosening your torso. Allow your body to bounce and shake. Let out any sounds that want to emerge. Shake your legs and swing your arms.

3. Once warmed up, stand (if you can, otherwise, sit) with your feet planted firmly on the floor or ground. Place your arms at your sides or lift them above your head.

4. Close your eyes and take slow deep breaths in and out.

5. Tune into your body. Feel your belly rise, and then your lungs fill as you inhale.

6. Listen to the sounds within you.

7. Take a deep breath, open your mouth, and then exhale with a loud sound.

Make your exhale big, a groan, a squeal, a guffaw, a scream, or any manner of strange sounds. There may be a variety of sounds changing from one moment to the next. Let them come out without judgment. Be open to the spontaneity of expression as much as possible.

8. Experiment with many sounds. After a while, you find the tone settles into a note that feels right for you, one you can sustain.

9. Allow yourself to sing this note as fully as possible. Reach for resonance. Relax your diaphragm, throat, and chest.

10. See if you can feel where the sound originates in your body. For example, is it from your throat, chest, belly, or head?

11. Try to let it come from your whole body at once. Move any seemingly disconnected body part until it's integrated into the sound you're making.

12. Let your body sway or move in synch with your singing tone.

After a while, the release of the tone settles to a natural place of quiet.

Notice how your body feels and what you can hear. And notice how present you feel. Write or draw in your journal to process and capture this new insight. Feel the flow of creativity often released by this resonance exchange with your 5ᵗʰ Chakra.

Ignite Your Creativity

When you can't find space and time to Phone Home, get out your journal and write. As Anodea Judith tells us, writing is a form of communication that transcends time.

The 5ᵗʰ Chakra is more than about communication with others. Writing in your journal is your chance to converse with yourself. Journaling lets you express pent-up energy to clear your mind. The doors to your inner being, The House of You, open as you write.

Light spills into the darkness where you can acknowledge negative feelings and emotions. Then, you ignite your intuition, sparking ideas, insights, and creativity.

Here's how to get your 5th Chakra energy flowing:

1. Writing in longhand is best. Something magical happens when you put pen to paper. However, going digital with a keyboard works too.

2. Sit in silence and write. The words flow once you start writing. Say what you please. Journals are private. No one else gets to read what you write. And if you wish, you can tear up, burn, or delete writing that might be hurtful to others.

3. Journaling helps you write out your feelings if you struggle with on-the-spot discourse. Then they won't stay bottled up inside.

4. When you have simmering frustration and anger, writing helps you keep a cooler head. A confrontation can become more of a conversation after safely venting your feelings.

5. Tap while reading out loud what you've written in your journal.

6. Make a note of the emotions and feelings emerging.

It takes time to bring our Throat Chakra into balance. And, with practice, our authentic truth comes through. First, prioritize your speaking style and tone of voice. Then, use your 5th Chakra to practice active listening to allow others the experience of being heard.

Chapter Nine

6ᵀᴴ CHAKRA
TAPPING FOR CLARITY

Clarity is not the place from which we begin
but rather the place at which we ultimately arrive.
—Victoria Labalme, *Risk Forward*

https://youtu.be/7_j2zTt5oho

SCAN ME

6ᵗʰ Chakra
Name: Third Eye, *Affirmation:* I See, *My Right:* To See
Themes: Empowered Intuition, Vision, Imagination, Lucidity,
Meditation, Trust, and Psychic Abilities
Primary Issues: Intuition and Imagination
Location in the Body: Brow
In The House of You: The Attic
Color Resonance: Indigo
Chakra Wisdom Crystal: Sodalite
Developmental Stage: Adolescence

Tapping for Clarity

We can sometimes drive ourselves crazy trying to make the simplest of choices. And some of us might even spend days agonizing over an important decision. This homeplay helps you access your intuition to find the clarity you seek.

Here are your steps for Tapping for Clarity:

1. Sit in a quiet place to avoid distractions and interruptions.

2. Take a nice deep breath. Feel your feet and wiggle your toes, and move your fingers.

3. Concentrate on your breath, noticing the rise and fall of your chest. Breathe deeper. Inhale, feeling your belly rise first, then fill your lungs. Breathe out in a long, slow exhale.

4. Continue to follow your breath as you begin to relax.

5. Place one hand on your heart. Notice where stress sits in your body, the areas of tension, discomfort, and unease.

6. With your hand on your Sacral Chakra, right below your navel, tap with two fingers of your other hand on the eyebrow point, your 6th Chakra, the Third Eye.

7. Focus on the issue at hand or the decision you must make.

8. Read the following script out loud as you tap. Add your own words, phrases, thoughts, feelings, and emotions. Tap while expressing what's going on for you.

Tapping Script

Ugh, this is so hard.
I wish I could make up my mind.
It's overwhelming.
I have to figure this out.
I can't decide.
This is maddening.
What should I do?
This indecision is making me crazy.
I wish I could see the outcome.
Which way do I go?
What direction do I choose?
I should be able to do this.
Why can't I do this?
I'm so stuck.
I'm such a loser.
A total mess.
I'm a big girl.
I'm supposed to be able to do this.
I help other people all the time.
At work.
At home.
What's wrong with me?
I'm unsure.
I wish I could know for certain.
What if I make a mistake?
What then?
I can't sleep.
I need to think about this.
I'm exhausted.
I gotta figure this out.
I'm so mad at myself for still being stuck on this.

9. Take another deep breath. Keep tapping your eyebrow point and envision the color, Indigo, a deep purplish blue.

10. Tap and ask for inner guidance.

Tapping Script

What do I need to know?
What do I need to learn?
What am I afraid of?
What am I missing?
What else do I need to see?

11. Once you feel a shift within you, breathe slowly and deeply. You don't have to fix it. Honor it. Tap using this script, or replace the words with your own.

Tapping Script

I'm just gonna honor how I feel.
I honor how frustrated I am.
I honor how much I've been through.
How much stress I've had.
And how hard this is.
I'm open to making the best decision for me at this time.
I don't know what it looks like yet.
I feel good about it.
I'm open to getting a good night's sleep.
I can sleep on it.
I'm open to making a clear choice.
As I remain still and breathe.
I ask for insights and ideas.
And I'm open for my intuition to guide me.

12. Take another nice deep breath and check in with your body. Often your stress level, physical tension, and discomfort are less.

However, if your level is still high or another emotion emerges, keep tapping and breathing. You don't need to say any words. The tapping itself lowers the intensity.

13. At bedtime, if your issue is still unresolved, tap again on any remaining nagging thoughts with the following script. Then, enjoy a good night's sleep.

Tapping Script

I've been so worried about this.
It's been on my mind.
And it's been a lot.
There's nothing I can do about it at night.
I'm ready to sleep well.
Wake up refreshed.
And have a clearer head tomorrow.
I'm open to inspiration.
Getting ideas.
And insights.
As I sleep.

Awaken feeling rested, restored, and inspired. Be sure to keep a notepad handy for writing down intuitive insights and ideas.

Isn't it amazing to wake up with an answer you've been seeking? Your spirit has been waiting here for you, wanting to give you access to Source energy.

Chapter Ten

7ᵀᴴ CHAKRA MEDITATION WITH TAPPING

The meaning of *wisdom* for me is recognizing the moment
when what you *know* aligns perfectly with what you *feel*.
—Oprah Winfrey, *The Wisdom of Sundays*

https://youtu.be/qHRpM0Ndozs

SCAN ME

7ᵗʰ Chakra
Name: Crown, *Affirmation:* I Understand, *My Right:* To Know
Themes: Empowered Wisdom, Fulfillment, Spiritual Connection,
and Enlightenment
Primary Issues: Enlightenment, Spiritual Connection, and Wisdom
Location in the Body: Top of the Head
In The House of You: The Stargazer Deck
Color Resonance: Violet
Chakra Wisdom Crystal: Amethyst
Developmental Stage: Throughout Life

Meditation with Tapping

Opening the 7th Chakra requires strengthening our ability to get still and focus. And meditation is an ideal way to access your gifts of intuition, spiritual connection, and the wisdom of your Higher Self. Give meditation a chance to understand pain, lower anxiety, and improve focus. Turn down your mind-chatter and invite mindfulness, connection, and bliss.

Oh no, not meditation. Do I have to?

I know. The mere word, meditation, may send you running. Perhaps you're thinking, *no thanks.*

Nah, Sandy, that's okay. I'd rather skip ahead to the next chapter and sit this one out.

There's too much to do, and it's hard to stop thinking. I don't know about you; I've never been able to make my mind go blank. How can we release the tension of our day and sit still? How do we turn off our brains? No worries. There are many forms of meditation, including walking or prayer. The following exercise is a combination of basic meditation and tapping. And note how meditation is comparable to tapping; you can't do it wrong.

You may be thinking, *I don't have time for meditation.* Nevertheless, time expands when you slow down, even for a few minutes. I know it sounds woo woo. There aren't any more minutes in your day. However, when you meditate, time widens, and you accomplish more. Powerful insights abound when you make time for reflection and meditation.

Follow this process for Basic Meditation with Tapping:

1. Find a quiet place to sit where you won't be disturbed.

2. Play soft music if you prefer.

3. Set a timer. Start with a short time segment of five to ten minutes.

4. Sit in a chair with your feet on the floor, kneel, or sit on the floor. Be sure you can stay comfortable in that position for your designated time.

5. Close your eyes. Or focus on a candle flame, plant, photo, or rotating fan. Or look out the window at the trees and sky.

6. Start tapping. Notice your breath. Breathe in through your nose and out through your mouth.

7. Imagine your breath flowing through your heart as if your heart is breathing for you.

8. Try counting breaths. Inhale. Hold. Exhale. Aim to exhale twice as long as you inhale. For example, inhale for a count of four, hold for four and exhale for eight.

9. Keep breathing slow, gentle, and deep. Now scan your body for areas of discomfort, unease, or pain.

10. Inhaling, send healing energy to those uncomfortable spots in your body. And exhaling, release toxic tension.

11. It's inevitable for your mind to wander. When you notice yourself drifting, return to your breath and tap. Avoid self-judgment and fixation on wandering thoughts.

12. When ready, stop tapping and place your hands on your heart. If your eyes are closed, slowly open them. Bring your focus back to the room. Take another deep breath.

13. Check in with your body. How does it feel?

14. Record your thoughts and emotions in your journal.

15. You did it!

The practice is simple. Focus your attention. When your mind wanders, loop around and bring it back. Be kind to yourself.

Chapter Eleven

CHAKRA BALANCING

Anything is possible when you open your
connection to the Universe.
—Colette Baron-Reid

https://youtu.be/XCxasK9guXM

SCAN ME

Chakra Wisdom Crystal: Clear Quartz, Master Healer
Themes: Empowered Alignment of all Chakras, Body, Mind,
Emotions, and Spirit

Chakra Balancing

Yes, we're meditating again. The way our energy system works, chakra clearing isn't a one-and-done process. It's more of a rinse-and-repeat routine. Throughout life, we keep uncovering, clearing, and healing chakra blocks. Like layers of an onion, there's another more profound revelation every time we peel away a hidden block. Epiphanies and divine aha moments move the negative energy. Are you up for the challenge? The more you practice tapping and meditation, the easier it gets. And your life transforms.

Here's your process for a Chakra Balancing Meditation:

1. Sit in a quiet place where you are undisturbed. If possible, place your feet flat on the floor with your spine in natural alignment from tailbone to crown. Or you can recline on a bed, couch, or floor.

2. Put one hand on your heart and tap with your other hand.

3. Take three slow, deep breaths. On the fourth breath, imagine your breath moving in a circle, in and out, through your heart. Inhale in through your nose and into your heart. Exhale out from your heart and through your mouth. Continue with three more slow, easy breaths.

4. Breathe deeper, filling your belly and then your lungs. Breathe in for a count of six, hold for four, and exhale for ten. Repeat three times.

5. Release tension from your body from head to toe. Relax your forehead, brows, cheeks, and chin. Let go of tightness in the back of your head, neck, and shoulders. Continue down your body through your upper and lower back, chest and torso, abdomen, hips, legs, knees, ankles, feet, and toes.

6. Keep breathing soft and slow. Feel your feet, wiggle your toes.

7. Continue tapping. Envision external chakras extending out from the bottom of your feet. They resemble cables pushing through the floor, the foundation, and into the ground.

8. Breathe and tap as you imagine chakra cables traveling deeper, all the way to the core of Mother Earth. Receive her beautiful,

warm, red energy, and see it rise back through the layers of earth and pool at your feet.

9.   Feel the warmth wrap around your feet. Embrace this healing empowerment energy traveling up your legs, knees, and hips to your pelvis. You're safe and supported in your 1st Chakra energy.

10. Tap as the energy flows into the on-fire orange of your 2nd Chakra, right behind your navel, where all your wants, needs, and desires swirl. And mixed in the fire are your negative emotions.

11. Energy continues to move up into the bright yellow light of ten thousand suns. Your Solar Plexus Chakra holds your power to act on your dreams and desires.

12. The energy enters the bright spring green of your 4th Chakra, your Heart. Send this healing green energy out to every cell of your body. Let it nourish every part of your being.

13. Now see with your inner eyes a bright white light bringing manifestation energy into you from Source.

14. Entering through your Crown Chakra, the light turns violet, bringing wisdom and spiritual enlightenment.

15. The violet energy deepens into Indigo at the 6th Chakra. Your Third Eye sparks your ideas, insights, and intuition.

16. Cascading into the blue of the 5th Chakra, the Throat, strengthens the power of your voice and listening skills.

17. Flowing now into the blue-green of the High Heart, manifesting speaking truth for all.

18. And back to the Heart Chakra, where manifestation energy meets empowerment energy. You're balanced and complete, a human with a divine spirit, a soul in human skin.

19. Place both hands on your heart, and take a deep breath. Bring in a sense of appreciation, gratitude, and love. Know that you are one with the Conscious Universe. You are in it, and you are of it. Feel the warmth, safety, and protection from below and universal love from above.

20. When you're ready, come back to the here and now. Look around. What stands out? What's different? Do things look brighter? Where do you see beauty? Hold the sense of love and appreciation as you continue your day or drift off to sleep.

Once you've practiced this tapping meditation, you can repeat it with ease. Envision each chakra color lighting up within you. Let it clear away anxiety, fear, and self-doubt, and quiet your inner critic. You are freeing your empowerment energy to help you manifest your dreams.

Shine Your Best Life

Continue to unblock your chakras and transform your life.

Additional Meditation Techniques

https://youtu.be/q0RjopJa8jA

SCAN ME

Creativity

Take a mind vacation while you focus on one activity:

- cooking, art, crafts, gardening, music, sewing, knitting
- organizing, interior decorating
- washing dishes, ironing, raking leaves

Writing

A. Powerful Connection to Your Higher Self

1. Put pen to paper. You can use electronics, your laptop, tablet, or phone. However, magic happens when you write longhand.

2. Sit in a comfortable place without disturbances. Choose a journal, notebook, or sketchpad, and explore using colored pens, pencils, and markers.

3. When you're not sure where to start, do a *mind dump*. Write down the thoughts in your head. Keep writing, even if it's a to-do list or nonsensical. At some point, you may notice a thought thread or theme. Go from there and continue writing. Doodle-draw and let your inner creativity flow onto the page.

4. When seeking clarity on an issue or idea, begin by writing a simple question.

    > *What do I need to know about this situation?*
    > *What would happen if I said yes? What's the downside?*

    Remember, your private journal is where nobody gets to see what you've written unless you choose to share it.

5. Write down your inner critic's argument.

6. Answer it with your written rebuttal. Thank your critic for bringing this issue to your attention. Remember, it's trying to protect you.

Go Deeper:

While tapping, read back what you wrote. Tapping clears residual negative thoughts, reaffirming the positive.

B. Create Affirmations

Circle three words or phrases in your journal entry. Starting with *"I am,"* create positive affirmations from the words you circled and place them in view throughout your day. Then, tap as you read them.

When inspiration accompanies your writing, you strike gold. Insights from your private journal can evolve into published works. Most authors, columnists, podcasters, bloggers, and poets start or end their days with journaling.

C. The Wisdom of Trees

1. Go outside. Bring a small notebook or journal and a pen.

2. Sit under a tree and feel safe while grounded in nature.

3. Breathe. Feel the breeze, notice branches swaying, and watch clouds floating across the sky. If you're near water, observe its flow. Look for birds, flowers, animals, and other critters.

4. When your mind wanders, breathe. Come back to nature.

5. Write down what comes to mind before it wanders.

Spirit Walking

1. Go out for a walk without a plan or destination. When you come to a point where you need to decide which way to go, pause. Tune into Spirit.

2. Let your inner guide choose your next step.

3. Avoid overthinking. Follow your intuition, that gut instinct, and see where it takes you.

4. Employ all your senses and observe the environment. What do you see, hear, smell, feel, and taste?

5. Watch for signs from Spirit, your angels, and guides. Notice feathers, coins, butterflies, birds, and animals.

6. Look for beauty wherever you go.

Reading Oracle Cards

Wouldn't it be cool if we could pick up the phone and call the Universe? Well, Oracle cards give us a direct link to Spirit. Use these divination cards to stimulate your inner knowing.

1. Before meditating, ask Spirit an open-ended question.

    What do I need to know about this issue or person?
    What do you want to show me before I start my day?
    What should I focus on as I go to sleep tonight?

2. Shuffle the cards. Pull one from the top, middle, or bottom.

3. Look at the image on the card, noticing what stands out to you. Then, read the message in the guidebook.

4. Find one word, phrase, or sentence that resonates with you.

5. Meditate and write in your journal.

A note about reversed cards: Sometimes, the card you pull is upside down. Don't fret. It's a potent hug from the Universe, known as a protection card, a signal to pay close attention to its message. Some oracle deck guidebooks include a protection message for each card. When you pull a reversed card, read only that message.

Praying

1. You can pray anywhere, anytime, out loud, or in silence.

2. Follow my client Eileen's lead from the story in Chapter Eleven of *The Woo Woo Way.* Pray and tap. It keeps you grounded in your body while connecting to God, Source, Universe.

3. A powerful prayer to start or end a mediation is The Serenity Prayer. It helps encourage acceptance, courage, and inner wisdom.

The Serenity Prayer

God grant me the serenity
To accept the things I cannot change;
Courage to change the things I can;
And wisdom to know the difference.

Recordings

A. Guided Meditation

Relax and follow the narrator's prompts. Discover how your mind's chatterbox tends to quiet faster with guided meditation. You may also search YouTube and Google for many free audio and video meditations, including mine. And there are great downloadable apps for your phone or smart device.

B. Narrated Tapping

Ignite your inner vision with the help of a narrator. The grounding effect of tapping lets you express and release feelings and emotions. The visualization can lead to profound epiphanies, self-empowerment, and transformation.

Go Deeper:

1. Finish your meditation with journaling, regardless of your form.

2. Take a few minutes to write, draw, or doodle.

3. Get down the insights and ideas, even if they don't make sense.

4. Put a pen, pencil, or crayon to paper.

5. Let the wisdom of your Higher Self pour onto the page.

Resources

https://youtu.be/RC5tG3vRZT4

SCAN ME

As an education junkie, I value lifelong learning. After attending numerous workshops and conferences and gathering hundreds of books, I offer you this sampling from my influential mentors and role models.

Books

The Tapping Solution: A Revolutionary Solution for Stress-Free Living by Nick Ortner thetappingsolution.com and The Tapping Solution App: Thetappingsolutionapp.com

The Tapping Solution for Weight Loss & Body Confidence: A Woman's Guide to Stressing Less, Weighing Less, and Loving More by Jessica Ortner thetappingsolution.com

Bliss Brain and *Mind to Matter: The Astonishing Science of How Your Brain Creates Material Reality* by Dawson Church, PhD, founder, EFT Universe
eftuniverse.com

Tapping into Wealth and *Unblocked: A Revolutionary Approach to Tapping into Your Chakra Empowerment Energy to Reclaim Your Passion, Joy, and Confidence* by Margaret Lynch Raniere, author, speaker, personal development coach and trainer
margaretlynchraniere.com

Spiritual Arousal: Intimate Poetic Verses, Connections With Your Heart And Soul by Ray Justice
rayjustice.com

The Cancer Cookbook, Food For Life by Roxanne Koteles, chef, certified Whole Health Educator and Coach
foodwisdomrx.com

Eastern Body Western Mind and *Charge and the Energy Body* by Anodea Judith, therapist, and public speaker on the chakra system, body-mind, somatic therapy, and yoga
anodeajudith.com

The Shadow Effect by Debbie Ford (diseased), Deepak Chopra, and Marianne Williamson, best-selling authors and internationally acclaimed leaders in the field of new thought
theshadoweffect.com

The Power of Now and *A New Earth* by Eckhart Tolle, German-born spiritual teacher and self-help author
eckharttolle.com

Physician Heal Thyself by Seema Khaneja, MD, physician, educator, coach, and founder of Coaching for Inner Peace and Shanti Academy
CoachingForInnerPeace.com

The Wisdom of Sundays: Life-Changing Insights from Super Soul Conversations by Oprah Winfrey, American talk show host, television producer, actress, and philanthropist

The Body Keeps the Score: Brain, Mind, and Body in the Healing of Trauma by Bessel van der Kolk, MD, physician and researcher
besselvanderkolk.com

Why Woo Woo Works and *The Five Side Effects of Kindness* by David R. Hamilton, PhD, former biochemist and pharmaceuticals developer, speaker, trainer, and author of eleven books
drdavidhamilton.com

You Are the Placebo and *Becoming Supernatural* by Dr. Joe Dispenza, International lecturer, researcher, corporate consultant, and educator
drjoedispenza.com

Wild and *Tiny Beautiful Things* by Cheryl Strayed, writer, podcast host
cherylstrayed.com

The Beauty of Living Twice by Sharon Stone, award-winning actress and human rights activist
IG @SharonStone

The Way of Integrity by Martha Beck
marthabeck.com

Messages from Spirit and *The Map* and *Uncharted* and *Remembering the Future* by Colette Baron-Reid, best-selling author, internationally-acclaimed Oracle expert, spiritual intuitive, personal transformation thought leader, educator, and speaker.
Host of Inside the Wooniverse podcast
colettebaronreid.com

A Cure for Emma by Julie Colvin, publisher, book project coach, and retreat facilitator
juliecolvin.com

Brilliant Breakthroughs for the Small Business Owner by author and CEO Maggie Mongan
brilliantbreakthroughs.com

Mind over Platter by Rosa Smith-Montanaro (Coach Rosa), Creator-Host of *Coffee with Coach Rosa,* training and workshop coordinator at rochesterworks.org
coachrosa.com

The Energy Codes: The 7-Step System to Awaken Your Spirit, Heal Your Body, and Live Your Best Life by Dr. Sue Morter
drsuemorter.com

More Mentors

Fiona Orr, Fiona Orr Coaching, Epic Life Coach
fionaorr.com

Arden Reece, Creative artist, visionary, and founder of the Color Fluency™ Method and Color Mystery School, a program and community focused on integrating the wisdom of color
ardenreececolor.com

Cindy Childress, PhD, Childress Business Communications, The Expert's Ghostwriter, book writing coach, and recipient of the Gold Award from the American Business Awards 2022: Company of the Year in Media & Entertainment
cindychildress.com

Becky Norwood, Spotlight Publishing House™, book self-publishing expert and creator of Bestselling authors
spotlightpublishinghouse.com

Maggie Mongan, Master Business Coach, Author, and Marketing Visibility Partner with Spotlight Publishing House
brilliantbreakthroughs.com

Lynn Thompson, Copy Editor, Living on Purpose Communications and Podcast
theonpurposepodcast.podbean.com

Experience more with Sandy

Be a part of Sandy's growing community. Subscribe to receive Sandy's email newsletters, where she shares stories with insights from her book and life journey. Be the first to know about upcoming programs. https://www.sandyevenson.com/

Book a Discovery Clarity Strategy Call
https://calendly.com/sandyevenson

ACCREDITATIONS

A. Coaching Certifications

    1. Master Faculty Coach at Margaret Lynch Raniere
       Intuitive Chakra Mastery
       Tapping Into Wealth
       Super Coach
       Excellence in Transformational Coaching Award

    2. Brittany Watkins
       Tapping For Weight Loss

    3. Collette Baron-Reid
       The Invision Process
       Oracle Guide

B. Brand Ambassador with BOOM by Cindy Joseph Cosmetics

C. Cohost of *Our Empowered Voices Podcast* with Coach Kay Walker

Ego says, "Once everything falls into place, I'll feel peace!"
Spirit says, "Find your peace, and then
everything will fall into place."
—Marianne Williamson